RAW
LEADERSHIP

RAW
LEADERSHIP

Awaken Your Power Within

Victoria Hargis

momma bear publishing

Palmetto
PUBLISHING GROUP

2nd Edition

ISBN-13: 978-0692532447
ISBN-10: 0692532447

*This book is dedicated to my eldest son Douglas,
who was there through most of it.*

*His brother, Davey's seizures, his dad's murder, and all the
struggles and difficulties that formed the mosaic of our lives
helped form the man you grew into... I could not give you
what I wanted then and you have no need of it now.*

*You were my first born, my shining star,
even when you did not feel it.*

*I am extremely honored to have had
the privilege of being your mom.*

I could not have done it without you - the book or my life.

Table of Contents

I was compared to a mother last week
All compassion and no fierce
And fierceness is what is required
In this situation.

Introduction

Without recognizing the value of what I was receiving at the time, I spent over a decade in intense trial by fire training to develop into a leader. I used the events that I call "mommabear moments" to propel me forward. It is my hope that my experiences can help you frame your own leadership training that is already in process and help you take your next steps to awaken your power within.

When I turned thirty I was expecting to have the best years of my life. I was married with two beautiful kids. Doug was seven and David was three. We had bought a house, my husband had a great job, and I was teaching in the local school district.

Within nine months the trajectory of my life dramatically shifted. My father died, my husband was murdered, and my youngest son inexplicably began having constant, debilitating seizures.

It is my hope that some of my experiences will benefit you and that the story of my son can be a blessing in your life.

Early one morning, seizures threw my son David to the floor. In shock, I lifted my blond-haired, blue-eyed angel in my arms and carried him out to meet the ambulance.

It happened again just seven days later. Each progressive week it happened over and over with escalating speed.

This acceleration overwhelmed me with fear. My young son David reached a point where he was having over sixty seizures a day and had to wear a helmet to protect his head. There were times where I had to leave the grocery cart in the aisle, full of groceries, while I carried my son to the emergency room to get his face stitched up from the latest attack, which would slam his face into the cart, or the floor, or any other object that happened to be around when his brain began its relentless misfiring.

Over 10,000 times that first year, bloody and beaten, I saw him pick himself up over and over to start again. And even as I write that number, I still cannot understand how he could begin again each time. If I had not witnessed his journey, I would have said it was impossible!

He broke his nose more than once. One type of seizure would slam him forward or backward, almost as if an outside force was slamming against the back of his knees like a cruel hoax. The only time he was safe was when he was in bed at night. The stress that the anticonvulsants put on his body caused him to regress. He was back in diapers and seemed to not be thinking clearly.

He seemed so battered and beaten, but still had a spark of life in him. In his desire to regain some control over his life, he told me confidently one day that he was no longer David but wished to be called Davey.

This book is about Davey and how he became my greatest mentor, teaching me how to live abundantly and to step into my innate leadership.

I spent so much time worrying for the future of my two boys.

Doug, my seven year old, started licking his lips as a nervous habit. He walked around for the next few years with a chapped mouth and an inch of redness from his tongue licking the surface of his face. He wouldn't talk about it to me or his counselor. He seemed out of reach to me and I believed the guilt he felt for his father's death and his brother's injury, even though he was not responsible for either event, was tearing him up inside.

Davey's misfiring brain would accelerate unrestrained until it collapsed from utter exhaustion. I was told that the children who develop this type of seizure disorder were usually institutionalized at some point because it became too much for their parents to manage. I was told there were no options for a cure, but I heard of an institute for brain-injured kids in Philadelphia that might offer a cure.

After sitting on a waiting list for thirteen months, feeling hopeless and exhausted, the parents of the brain injured children, who had appointments the same week as I did, sat in a chilly fifty-five degree lecture auditorium at an institute in Philadelphia for three days while the staff watched the kids. What they had to teach us was too important to miss, so cold was used to keep us alert and a caution that if anyone fell asleep they would lower the temperature.

No one fell asleep as we listened for hours every day about how the brain works and what it takes to bring wellness back to our children. The information they provided was priceless. On the last day, each parent and child was given a list of what they had to do every day for the next three months. We were warned that if we missed a day we would be kicked out of the program, but we left with hope. This was something I had not dared to think or even dream about for the previous two years.

Having a child with a brain injury is hard, and it is almost impossible to describe the utter hopelessness that can be triggered. The resignation that your child will never play like others is accompanied by an anxious preoccupation with watching how they are doing every moment and the grief over everything that they don't seem to be learning. You see the ever widening gap between their chronological age and their neurological age.

We went home and started the program. The first event each day consisted of a half mile of crawling on his belly, a half mile of creeping on his hands and knees, and twelve sets of patterning. Patterning involved Davey lying on a table while three adults moved his head, arms, and legs in a cross pattern to create the neuro pathways for correct movements. If he had a seizure, we would take a break until he recovered and then start again. He also had to do masking 60 times a day to increase his respiratory function. It made for a full day every day.

Three months later we went back for a checkup. Davey seemed to be growing faster than before. The circumference of his head and chest, and his height and weight, were measured. Children with brain injuries typically grow more slowly.

None of the children in our group had the exact same symptoms. Some were blind or deaf. Others couldn't read, walk, or talk and they ranged in age from two to twenty-one. All their parents were exhausted, but fully committed to finding a way to improve their children's situations.

At the first program reunion, I saw kids reading who didn't have a hope of reading just three months earlier. We got our instructions for the next six months and left more hopeful than we had been in a long time. For Davey there was more creeping, crawling, brachiating exercises, and weaning him off his anticonvulsants.

After a short time on the program, he gained back some of his developmental milestones and got back his impish smile. He grew and prospered in spite of all the seizures. He became tall and strong.

He was filled with love, a sense of justice, and deep empathy for others. This program continued for five years. Davey became totally drug free and seizure free during the day. He began to write and he ran three miles daily, and up to eight miles on Saturdays. He worked hard every day. Sometimes he would get so tired that he would fall asleep on the toilet, hugging his beloved bunny blanket.

We studied together, learning Greek and Latin root words for vocabulary, French for when he could travel, math, writing, reading, and common etiquette. In the process, he taught me love and we mastered not giving up, even when the way was long and seemingly impossible.

After five years on the program we were advised by the staff at the Institute to take a 6 month break and see what being a normal family was all about. Shortly after starting this break, my second husband, James was having health issues. He developed diabetic neuropathy and went blind. During the next few years we worked on healing James with the intention of going back on the program for Davey when that happened. James got his vision back after a number of operations. And it was with great sadness that I was not able to get Davey back on the program.

Davey passed away on January 5, 1992, at the age of thirteen, but he lives on in the lessons he taught me and the gifts he gave me. Davey, a beloved son and brother had conquered many of the difficulties that plagued his life and was not able to take the last steps into wellness.

I focused this book on leadership because I came to believe that I originally had the concept of leadership all turned around.

RAW LEADERSHIP

Leadership is not some magic thing that some people have; it is innate in all of us. When we pulled ourselves up and took our first steps we were demonstrating our ability to reach inside ourselves and take the steps necessary to reach a goal that is the definition of a leader. We were a success magnet and we were able to reach our goals to crawl to walk, to run, to learn whatever foreign language is around us. And over time we learn how to not be that person we were and to fit into the family, culture and society in which we were born.

I saw that leadership is primarily about leading ourselves. This book is about becoming a self-aware leader, one who is authentically connected to their purpose. This is about getting that innate leadership turned back on by reaching into ourselves and rekindling the flame that has dimmed or gone out.

There are specific milestones along the way to becoming an authentically self-aware leader, and the chapters in this book point the way. At the end of each chapter are questions that will help you begin your journey. Stop and journal about the questions and thoughts you may have, as they come up.

Note: In this book I use the Universe, God, Source, and the Creator interchangeably. I'm sure the Creator does not mind and they all work for me. Please use the term that resonates with you that refers to the divine.

CHAPTER ONE

Being Mindful

Staying Present

We think and do things automatically in life. It is the automatic thoughts and actions that make up the ego and keep us from being mindful. The ego is not you! It is, in fact, a highly sophisticated reflex response with a whole range of different responses that are triggered by different environments. Unlike something like the blinking reflex, which is hardwired from birth, the ego is flexible and can learn responses that work better for our lives. The ego is a set of learned reflexes. This is great because it allows us to adapt and learn new behaviors.

Imagine for a moment if you had to relearn how to climb a set of steps every time you encounter a new set. Having a learned response for stairs is a good thing. And so it is with many things in our lives. It is not so helpful when working with others and yet we respond automatically if we get triggered. This happens automatically most often on a sub conscious level. A look, a scent, a comment, body type or really anything that comes into our brain can trigger a knee jerk response.

Unfortunately, the ego is not infallible. A traumatic or antisocial experience in your past can leave your responses permanently warped and unadapted for your current life. It does not even need to be traumatic it can be any event that creates an automatic response that is not resourceful.

The ego is so in control of our thoughts that it can seem that the ego is who we are. You might say "I am angry" or "I am happy" or "I am sad", but that is not entirely accurate. You *experience* the feeling of anger, happiness or sadness triggered by a certain situation or person, but it isn't intrinsic to who you are - you have *acquired* that response due to a prior experience, and you can unlearn it. You are NOT the emotions you experience, the emotions you feel.

The only part of you that is really you is the part that is aware. What that means is, until you become aware of how you are creating the responses you are having to events and people, you are living life on an unconscious level.

Most people live their lives on autopilot, not being truly themselves, but being controlled by the automated responses of their ego. This might be fine if your life and default attitude is bright and happy. Why would you want to wake up from that? Unfortunately, most egos are fearful, sad, lonely or bitter, and their lives are spent in a nightmare of disappointment which they inflict on the next generation by their behavior.

The ego's fear of the future, and replaying past *failures*, keep us stuck in the life we are living and prevent us from moving into the life we were born to live. The ego's job is to keep us safe by making us afraid of trying new things or from challenging our personal beliefs.

A point to note: your ego is not your enemy, it helped you to survive and learn. However, it was not meant to be the ruler of your life. The ego makes a great servant and a lousy boss. It will attempt to keep you unaware and knows everything that you do.

In women, it seems the ego is especially vulnerable to fears of not measuring up. We compare ourselves with ad images, obsess over losing baby weight and believe that if we don't have the perfect skin, body or life we are not good enough. We worry how we might be judged for our mothering skills if our children are too loud or too quiet. We tend to fall into the trap of measuring our self-worth based on our physical attractiveness and our ability to care for other's needs adequately.

Ironically, some of the harshest critics are sometimes fellow struggling women. I would like to propose that we are more than just our physical bodies or our external circumstances and challenge women to feel a sense of wonder and gratitude for themselves just as they are. They do not need to work themselves into exhaustion to earn their right to be in the world. Once they stop and breathe, it becomes possible to form an inner sense of connection to the divine, awaken the imagination, and begin to consciously fulfill their destiny.

You can operate as a leader or you can operate as a victim the choice is yours. Identifying as a victim in any part of your life means you may be in a mindset where you will not assert your power. This, sadly, may set you up to repeat your previous circumstances again and again.

Note: the ego will tell you that you are not operating like a victim. Become aware of the number of times you complain about something in your life or someone in your life. In those complaints you will find where in your life you are acting like a victim.

We all see the world through our own lens. Our world is reflective of the beliefs we hold. We project onto the world what our parents, teachers, peers, or our religion modeled for us. Much of what we were taught is good for survival purposes, like looking both ways before crossing a street, but we also pick up the harmful programming of prejudices and irrational fears.

Until we are willing to examine what we believe on an unconscious level, we will be running old programming without being aware of why our life is not working.

I am reminded of the story of a daughter who watched her mother cut off both ends of the ham before she placed the pieces into the roasting pan for Easter dinner. The daughter asked the mother why she was doing that. The mother replied that her mom had always done it that way, so she did too. When the daughter checked with her grandmother, she learned that the ham hadn't fit in the pan so her grandmother had cut off the ends to make it fit.

Where are you needlessly cutting off the ends to make something fit in your unconscious belief system? Maybe it is time to look at what you believe and see if it is in line with who you are. Your unconscious beliefs could be robbing you of the ability to see your purpose. We must all be present and accounted for to create the world we want. Are you willing to do this self-work?

As long as our unconscious beliefs filter reality for us, we cannot be genuinely in the present. The past is coloring our experiences in a biased way.

What if we embraced all that life has to offer in the present moment and looked for things to be grateful for in that moment? How would your life change if you practiced gratitude in the moment?

I learned a valuable lesson from Davey when I brought his new helmet to him. He was playing in the backyard with his brother. There were few places on earth where he was safe, and the backyard was no exception. Seizures often came without warning and they would smash him into any available object.

On this afternoon, I interrupted his play to showcase the bright, shiny, yellow helmet that had been bought to protect his head. I wanted to give him as normal a life as I could, while still keeping him safe. The helmet would allow him more freedom.

Davey was just being a kid, playing and having fun. When he came over to me I pretended to be enthusiastic as I showed him all the cool aspects of wearing this fabulous protective helmet, all the while cringing on the inside over how hard I anticipated his life would be.

As I watched him receive the gift, I saw something completely contradictory to the fear I was feeling. I saw hope and excitement on his face. As I buckled the strap under his chin, he tried to peek around me and his eyes lit up. With a big playful grin he asked, "Where's my motorcycle?"

Right there, in that moment, Davey taught me that life is what we make it.

I imagine that Davey's recollection of that moment must have been something like this:

> I was playing with, my brother, Doug in the backyard. We were running, climbing the swing set, and digging in the sandbox. Mom came and brought me a yellow helmet. She put it on my head and I kept trying to look around her cuz I knew that a helmet always came with a motorcycle. I wanted to ride my motorcycle! Mom looked sad even though she was smiling. When I asked her where my motorcycle was, she almost cried. I wonder why...

The ten years before Davey died were filled with great excitement. We watched Davey conquer the seizures and learn to read. We went on field trip adventures and got to do all the hopeful physical conditioning and breathing therapies together. These years were also filled with the numbing fear of not being able to bring him to total health and always wondering what else we could do to help him heal.

Life was really what Davey made of it; he never thought of himself as a victim. He just lived in the moment and he was happy. I was projecting all my fears about the future into the moment, which made me experience those same moments with sadness and fear.

What was the difference? How did we see it so differently? We begin our life like an innocent sponge, ready to soak up all the world has to teach us, with no filter. How our parents spoke to us became part of our inner voice. And how we speak to our children becomes part of their inner voice. We lift them up to spread their wings or we dishearten them, leaving them living small and crippled by their internal belief system.

We are born with the need to connect to others, our parents, our siblings and our world. It is one of the 5 basic needs that every human has and needs to have filled.

> *"Human beings are hard-wired with the impulse to share our ideas... and the desire to know we've been heard. It's all part of our need for community. That's why we're constantly sending out signals and signs. It's why we look for them from other people. We're always waiting for messages, hoping for connection... And if we haven't received a message, it doesn't always mean it hasn't been sent to us. Sometimes it means we haven't been listening hard enough."*[1]

Our ego, the unconscious patterns that we created as we grew can prevent us from connecting and fulfilling that need.

Being mindful requires that we take a step back from external input and check in with ourselves. We are limited by the version

---

1 *Tim Kring, screenwriter, Touch TV Series 2012-2013*

of our own brain's reality map. If we want to become leaders in our own lives, we need to examine our map of reality. We need to see the places in our map that haven't been updated to fit who we want to be and what we want to have in our lives.

For example, reactions to a situation could actually be reactions to old memories. Entertain the idea that no one can make you angry against your will. We choose either consciously or unconsciously to have a particular emotion. When we experience something we write our stories back on to our map and reinforce our old world views. If we do not become aware of what is driving our reactions the map gets reinforced with the old beliefs. An emotional response out of proportion to the situation can occur either because we are connecting to a memory, or projecting a fear about the future onto the present.

It is very easy to project outward when a situation occurs.

Have you ever said "He made me so mad" or "He is such a ___"? If you have said or thought something like this, you were projecting your internal map of reality on a situation. Look for the possible messages that you didn't have the eyes to see before.

Be ruthless in demanding the truth from yourself. Only a true, accurate perspective of your starting point can allow you to be mindful and get what you want.

Staying in the present means we own all of our thoughts and feelings without filtering out the parts we think will not be acceptable to others. The world needs us to show up in every situation. All of us!

Takeaway:

Facing our old hurts and fears will help us to stop unconsciously projecting them onto current situations. Staying conscious of our feelings allows us to know our biases and refocus on our purpose.

When becoming a leader, staying in the moment is important, we must feel what we feel and face what it brings up in us. Doing so stops us from projecting onto another person and helps us heal. Awakening your power means you own your actions and your life. This is truly the only way we can stay connected to our purpose and in the present. Staying in the moment helps us by keeping us mindful and aware. When we are aware, we can change negative behavior patterns and create better results.

Stepping Stones:

What kind of world do you want to live in?

_____

_____

_____

_____

_____

What kind of impact do you want to have?

_____

_____

_____

_____

_____

_____

In what areas of your life are you already the person you want to be?

_____

_____

_____

_____

_____

_____

_____

In what areas of your life are you not yet the person you want to be?

_____

_____

_____

_____

_____

_____

What do you need to do to create the version of yourself that is who you want to be?

_____

_____

_____

_____

_____

_____

_____

In what areas are you letting your external circumstances shape and control who you present yourself as?

_____

_____

_____

_____

_____

What can you see or feel in this situation that will help you become more present?

_____

_____

_____

_____

_____

_____

Asking yourself these questions will start you on the path to becoming a leader with mommabear qualities.

CHAPTER 2

Seeing a Better Me

On the Road to "More Better"

I still have phrases in my vocabulary that Davey used, these have stuck with me over the years. One such term is "more better" and I find myself using and understanding this on an ever-deepening level. There is always something more and something better. We can always go deeper and learn to love better. Being a leader means that you are willing to be wrong and nothing will stop you from taking chances to reach your goal.

I discovered this when I decided to take Davey to The Institutes for the Achievement of Human Potential. They are leaders in their field helping brain injured children heal. For over fifty years, parents of brain-injured children have made the trek to their doors in order to find a way to heal their children.

The Institutes is a promise and a hope. It is there that I learned that life is not preordained, that it is a co-creative process that changes according to my actions. What we use grows, and what we don't actively use doesn't grow. If you want something "more better" in your life, then you must be willing to be wrong, to take a risk and try something different.

Some of the principles the Institutes teach are to help the brain-injured child grow to social, physical, emotional, and intellectual excellence. Figuring out what excellence means, and how to achieve it, was a five-year journey that set off a much longer and more encompassing search for the meaning of life.

The simple principles that we use to help heal a brain-injured child are the same tools that we use to heal ourselves and become the leader in our own life. In each of the areas or environments of my life, I needed to take a good look at where I was and see where I wanted to go. Then I had to learn and apply the skills that would bring me there.

Working within the confines of The Institutes' programs with Davey, we worked on the following environments in his life, working toward excellence in each of them:

Social Growth

Physical Growth

Emotional Growth

Intellectual Growth

For example: if I want physical excellence in my life, sitting on the couch watching Netflix or eating chocolate is probably not going to get me there. When I decided to get off the couch and start taking karate classes, it was not necessarily with the intention of achieving physical excellence; however, after taking several classes I decided to lose some weight.

I did a cleanse and lost some weight. Losing the weight gave me the belief that losing weight was possible and showed me that adding ten pounds per decade as we age is not necessarily the truth. The next year I decided to change my lifestyle and accept a healthier life. I lost over thirty pounds and kept them off. My belief changed as I moved forward. I would not have been able to envision losing thirty pounds the day I got up off the couch, but that small step took me to the place where that became plausible in my world view.

Where in your life would you like to reach farther? What is the nagging thought in the back of your mind? Do you wonder what unresolved wounds may be triggering you to have strong reactions to some people or comments?

Watching Davey grow into the person he became gave me a great foundation for my own journey. It was the small things that we did consistently that changed his quality of life. It did not happen overnight it took consistently reaching toward the goal every day. My first journey inward was in the early nineties triggered by Davey's death and yet it encompassed an intense desire to understand what it all meant. Why was I here? What was my purpose?

I experienced a lot of turmoil at the beginning of my journey. I did not have a support system. I got told I was grieving incorrectly and at one point got told I was going to hell because I was questioning what it all meant.

I turned to the companions of my childhood, my beloved books. I searched for meaning, I read everything I could get my hands on and spent time in meditation and on retreats. The answers didn't come easily. I didn't have exactly the right book to compare my experiences to. I read books like *The Road Less Traveled* by M. Scott Peck, *A Course of Miracles* by Helen Schucman, *The Hero's Journey* by Joseph Campbell, all of which provided some guidance, but I still felt lost. So after hitting one brick wall after another I shut down, figuring I had gotten it wrong again.

I already felt like a failure in so many areas of my life that this frustration came as no surprise. I spent many of the following years feeling numb and just going through the motions of living. I found it hard to connect with anyone. I even shut down my facial expressions not consciously but subconsciously reacting to the situation I was in. I did not have anything on the current map of reality I was operating off of to help me through the journey I was on. So I retreated inward going through the motions of living but really checked out.

What does it mean to consciously work on oneself? If we don't have the life we want, how do we go about getting it? Beginning to find the vibrant personality buried inside of you can be as simple as just letting yourself feel what is happening to you right now. Practice refocusing on staying present in the moment and really enjoying this day. Ask yourself if you really believe all the things you say you do. Then ask yourself why you believe that. To really know yourself and what part of yourself to work on next, you need to understand what currently drives your responses and actions in your life.

Before you can lead effectively and inspire others to follow, you have to dig deep within yourself and know yourself beyond your superficial conditioned beliefs. You need to have a deep understanding of, and ability and willingness to work through, your anger, pain, sadness, and unhappiness.

Begin to examine all the events in the mosaic of your life, acknowledge the feelings, heal them where needed, and then let the past go! If you do not yet have the life that you want, you are probably holding onto pain that happened to you in the past. Holding on to the hurt, pain and anger of the past is keeping you stuck and preventing you from the life you were born to have.

When I started my journey, it would have helped to have someone to bounce ideas and feelings off of. If there were people who thought I was sane and on an important journey, they did not reveal themselves to me. Being isolated made the journey much harder. My journey back then was one of knowing what I didn't want, not knowing what I did want. Being able to say I what I did want took more time.

For me, one of the ways I needed to grow was to reconnect to my inner child. When I was very young, I was extremely lonely. I did not know at the time that it was not normal to feel isolated for long periods of time, especially in a family of eight kids. My father struggled with bouts of rage, if we made too much noise or didn't do what he wanted he would erupt. I read books voraciously to escape. I liked biographies, adventures, or really anything I could get my hands on to learn about other cultures and ways of being. I hoped I would have another way of living when I was grown and had my own children.

In my family, intelligence was prized above everything else. When I was born, the doctor told my parents that I was re-tarded. As you might imagine, I was not exactly welcomed with open arms by my mother and father. My older sister took care of me from when she was just six, and it is my understanding that I was largely overlooked by the adults.

There are parts of my past that are hard to describe. It seemed normal to have a father that screamed and beat us. In one of my father's fits of rage when I was two, he picked me up and hurled me at the wall. My older sister told me years later that she thought I was dead when I hit the floor.

When I realized this was in my history, I could not reconcile it with my memories. I found myself carefully picking up my two year old grandchild to try to understand it. That memory finally came back in bits and pieces until I suddenly felt the pain that I must have experienced as a child when being thrown against a wall. It came back to me as a muscle memory that had me curled into a ball experiencing excruciating pain over a period of a couple of weeks.

Growing up, we were sent to bed at 6pm. Four of us slept in a very hot, small bedroom on two sets of bunk beds. The dresser didn't fit and sat in the hallway. Many nights we failed at our attempts to avoid angering my father. The sound of his ankles creaking on the stairs as he approached, and the sound of his belt being pulled free from his pants, heightened our fear.

My smart, younger sister would quickly pretend to be sleeping, but I remember wearing the welts across the back of my legs and the pain and humiliation of going to school with marks.

When trauma happens it is normal to segment the memory in order to protect who we are. It took a long time to get back those memories and reclaim little Victoria. There were also times where I felt that having more than one inner child meant that I was crazy and I worried that I was like Sybil (the women with multiple personalities). If that is the case with you, I want to remind you that it is normal to have as many inner children as you needed to survive your life.

What did I feel as I stood again
On little shaken legs
After being thrown
Like a piece of garbage
Against the wall.
I know I was not
The same person that
Was picked up in his angry hands,
Was it really only seconds ago?

Blasted by rage
Shaking like a
Frightened leaf
A small twig off
The family tree.
So I stood on shaking
Legs different than I was
Only a few short seconds ago.
The defiant demand that
I be seen, acknowledged
My spirit seeking to be heard
In a small two year old body
Ended with a smash and
A crumble.
And now I seek to understand
What it was that I felt
And who it was that I was
Before I was me.

I accepted trauma as the norm, I knew no other life. When I realized how *not normal* that was, initially I was angry, but I began to see there is tremendous value to having lived on the fringe. It allowed me to avoid being influenced by conventions or blindly following those trying to maintain their power. It allowed me to think for myself, to develop my own sense of the world, and to question my part in it early on. It helped me to be clear on what I believed. I felt free to challenge things that did not make sense and to think for myself.

Being on the fringe and trying the experimental approaches to healing meant that I had to be strong enough to do what needed to be done with minimal assistance. I was blessed with the church family that volunteered to help those first few months, however, I was able to manage Davey's therapies independently after the second visit to the Institutes. It was hard to accept that I needed help. When I give to others, I am now aware that receiving help can be hard on the recipient.

I learned there was strength in not being part of the world during those years when my only goal was healing Davey. Living that way allowed me the courage to journey within not once but twice. The first taught me many things the second one brought me home to myself.

> Doc had taught me the value of being the odd man out: the man who senses that there is an essential collective insanity to humans and who assumes the role of the loner, the thinker, and the searching spirit who calls the privileged and powerful to task. The power of one was based on the courage to remain separate, to think through to the truth, and not to be beguiled by conventions or the plausible arguments of those who expect to maintain power.[2]

I had been separated from others by choice sometimes, and then sometimes not by choice, I was constantly learning about connection to others and myself. I believe we have forgotten our connection to each other, that we have come from, and we are all pending return to, the same Source. What I had forgotten

---

2 Courtenay, Bryce. *The Power of One*. New York: Delacorte, 2005. Print.

along the way was that I was born magnificent, indeed we are all born magnificent and the journey is to reclaim that birthright.

What we believe is based on filters from our childhood. When we connect to the bigger vision of what we see as a possibility, we can create a reality that is "more better". And so it was with me as I started to remove filters. Connecting to the Source again, I began to see the bigger vision.

When the spirit begins to call you, it is an opportunity to heal and stop playing small. It is asking you to see the possibility of your own magnificence. You are wrong if you think that is referring to someone else. Suspend your grip on your current reality and dare to see different possibilities for yourself.

I was raised to put my needs last. If someone asked me what I wanted, I couldn't imagine what my actual needs were, and couldn't have articulated them even if I did know. I would often say that it didn't matter what we did or where we went because I would always find something to like in it. If I didn't, I could always go inside and think. I believed that only boring people are bored because there is always something to think about.

When trying to figure out what you like sometimes it helps to start by questioning the most elementary level of your physical state. Am I hungry? Am I thirsty? Am I cold? By connecting to our most basic needs, we can stay present in the moment. And being present is the fastest way to refocus on our purpose and allow us to love and be loved "more better".

Many of my mentors have been the children that have been in my life. My granddaughter Jacelyn is a quiet, reserved child who reminds me of me when I was little. She reminds me of the importance of being present.

Takeaway:

Having a vision of something better is the difference between being a victim and being a victor. Your inner child needs to know that there is something "more better" to look forward to out there. There is something "more better" out there, or should I say there is something "more better" inside each of us. The glimpse of other possibilities, which I saw in shows and read in books, kept that vision alive. Often it is not about the conditions we grew up in, but how we perceive them and react to them that make the difference in our life.

Stepping Stones:

What is your vision of what could be "more better" in your life?

_____

_____

_____

_____

_____

_____

_____

_____

_____

What is the new version of yourself that you want to reach for?

_____

_____

_____

_____

_____

_____

_____

_____

In what areas do you perceive life as happening "to" you?

_____

_____

_____

_____

_____

_____

What is preventing you from stepping into your new life?

_____

_____

_____

_____

_____

_____

CHAPTER 3

The Difficulty in Life is the Choice

Be Purpose-Filled
"The Difficulty in Life is the Choice."[3]

O nce we connect to our purpose, it doesn't matter what obstacles get in the way or how hard it is. We will keep going until we accomplish our outcome, even if it feels like the battle is all uphill.

We live with the consequences of every choice we make or refuse to make. I chose to take Davey to The Institutes to give him every opportunity to become who he was meant to be. The program sometimes felt almost impossible to be on.

---

3 Moore, George. *The Bending of the Bough; a Play in Five Acts.* Chicago: De Paul U, 1969. Print.

I was stretched beyond what I believed I was capable of accomplishing. It changed my life in so many ways. I learned how to endure and commit to a goal. I learned that possibilities lay only a small step outside my comfort zone. Doing the program was not comfortable or glamorous, but I knew it was Davey's only chance at a normal life.

There have been many times in my life that I thought I could not accomplish what was in front of me. When I was five, my baby brother died. I asked God for a blond-haired little boy with blue eyes that I could name David after my little brother. I was given the gift of Davey, who had a profound impact on my life. I grieved throughout his life time as I watched him struggle and conquer each obstacle and I measured how far he still had to go.

As I share his story in my presentations, I heal myself and help audience members who connect with his story. With the gift of Davey I was also given a mission. I needed to share that gift with the world, but for many years I did not know how. I felt crippled by my childhood and messages I had taken in that told me I had neither the right, nor the ability, to affect others.

Fast forward to today and I have broken free of those old beliefs. I am learning to share this gift with my audience and learning how to reclaim and own that my personal power are gifts given to me in the present. Recognizing the effect I was having on people by telling Davey's story took me a while it did not happen overnight.

I tell you this story to let you know that it doesn't matter how hard or big the obstacle is. If you have a clear purpose, it can help you choose to get up after you get knocked down. If you sometimes lose touch with your reason to fight, force yourself to get up and continue to fight until it becomes clear. Force yourself to do what you would do if you already felt that purpose. Ask yourself "What would it take to be the person that is filled with purpose?"

Where in your life are you letting real or imagined obstacles stop you from achieving your dreams? What if today you just started by taking the next step? Take one simple, little step toward your future. You don't have to climb the mountain in one day.

A shift in circumstances sometimes pushes us to make new choices, After five years on the program from The Institutes. With the condition of my second husband, James' health and advice from the doctors who strongly suggested that we take a break from the program we took what I thought would be a short 6-month break. James was developing diabetic retinopathy and slowly going blind, so we were told to take time to be a family and do something we really wanted to do together.

What immediately came to our minds was to buy some property and build a home in the country. We lived in a subdivision with houses built on top of each other. We decided to take six months and build a house on some property we had found just south of Burlington, Wisconsin.

It was during the time we were building the house; I almost went under from the stress. James had lost his job shortly after we started and while there was enough money to build the house there was little more. I was not sure if we could survive or not. It was during this time that I felt the most defeated in my life. Finishing the home took a backseat to the medical necessities of getting James' vision fixed so the six months turned into years.

We were not able to start Davey back on the program again and I felt it was my inability to communicate or motivate that led to Davey's death.

The grief from a number of events in my life during that time culminated in me feeling shattered. As I contemplated the pieces of my life that I had no ability to put back together, I felt that I had reached the absolute limit of what I was capable of enduring. I even seriously contemplated suicide; I felt like I had no hope left and I didn't know where I had gone wrong.

Who would I have been if I had made different choices along the way? How did some of those choices make me the person that I am? I lived a life outside of mainstream culture. Sometimes I refer to that time as "the time I lived in a vacuum" with only glimpses every now and then of normal. Did staying outside mainstream conventions help or hurt me?

The hardest thing I ever had to do was not going back on that program after the break. I lived in possibility for over five years and then felt like it was being taken away. There was a barricade between me and what I wanted for Davey.

I believed that my inability to get someone to hear what I was saying was what led to Davey's death. This belief drove me to become a speaker. My mission now is to master communication, which will allow me to share Davey's message about living abundantly with purpose and passion.

Takeaway:

Leaders don't back down from a challenge, either from themselves or from others. We make the best possible future we can with the tools at hand. We reach deep inside ourselves to accomplish things that may have seemed impossible. You can easily meet your own emotional needs, but only if you stop running away from your history.

If someone had told me what I was doing was a sacred journey and a necessary process, it would have been so much easier. I am telling you today that the journey of the self is the hardest thing you will ever embark on, but until you do, you will be living only half alive and wondering if this is all there is. There is treasure inside of you and you are the only one who can take the journey and discover it.

Stepping Stones:

In what areas of your life are you just coasting along?

_____

_____

_____

_____

_____

Where in your life do you feel uneasy?

_____

_____

_____

_____

_____

_____

What from your past haunts you?

_____

_____

_____

_____

_____

Are you ready to commit to doing the work that is necessary to free you from what has been holding you back?

_____

_____

_____

_____

_____

CHAPTER 4

That is Not Who I Am

Create an Empowering Relationship with Yourself

W e had healed Davey to the point where he did not have any daytime seizures and were finally able to send him to school. He still got them about every 3 weeks when he was in his bed at night sleeping, and I did not have to worry as much about him hitting his head or slamming his face into objects. He was safer, even if not completely healed. I could breathe a little, even though I had no ability to continue the program that had brought him so far. The financial resources were not available for me to run the twenty-four-hour program that was needed now.

Davey asked to go to school, and I agreed and enrolled him in the local middle school. He came home one afternoon, furious. Normally he would take an old broom handle and beat up the trash cans when he was angry with how life was going at school. There had been quite a bit of bullying. Reports of fish hooks in his lunch and kids being mean were common. James and I witnessed one boy tripping him on purpose in the hallway, as three teachers looked on silently. Most of the time Davey just handled it; this day was different. Some boys at school had ramped up the bullying to the point that they shoved him down in the bathroom at school. Davey was venting to me about how angry he was.

I attempted to give him advice on how to navigate the bully situation at school.

"Davey, I don't want you to fight, I don't believe in it, but if they push you or hit you or knock you down, I want you to DECK them."

"But, Mom, you don't understand... that is not who I am," an exasperated Davey informed me.

Only my sons can stop me in my tracks this way. I realized how well he knew who he was. Few people reach that level of self-knowledge even after living decades longer.

He made me realize in my own life how much easier it is to say what I am not, instead of saying what I am.

I began to ask myself questions about my perceptions. Who did I perceive myself to be and how was it different from what others saw?

I have always worked to clear up my perceptions about situations, to attempt to see things more clearly, but like everyone, I operate through the lens of my wounds. Being aware of that fact has caused me to bend over backward to give others the benefit of the doubt. This can also, unfortunately, mean that I sometimes enabled others to maintain their non-resourceful personal perceptions. I had some misguided idea that I always needed to avoid upsetting others.

Doing this caused me to maintain multiple belief systems about a situation at the same time, which was exhausting. As I was reading one morning, I realized that there were a number of perceptions that had not been serving me. One such perception was the one about gender. I had always had an issue with using the masculine pronoun when referring to both genders. I believed that leads to ambiguity and misunderstanding.

I had a conversation with one of my mentors, which triggered me along the same lines of gender. Although I believe he did not mean it the way I heard it, this conversation sent me down the rabbit hole, which in turn brought me back to the book A Course of Miracles again, and a better understanding of my own limiting perceptions.

A Course of Miracles was precious to me and one of the few books I've kept with me. However, one of the things that had always distracted me from what it was teaching was that it was written using only the masculine pronoun. I didn't feel included. I'm not a son; I'm a daughter of God. All the teachings refer to sons, which had made me feel out of place.

And yet, I learned that as long as I keep myself attached to my preconceptions, I cannot grow. Age, gender, height, hair color, attractiveness, etc. are all preconceptions that I needed to let go of. It is our attachments to the labels of man or women, tall, short, bald, beautiful, ugly, leader or not leader that keeps us stuck.

Where in your life are you letting your or someone else's perceptions and preconceptions hold you back? Where do you need to remove this distorted lens?

We all get feedback every day, whether in the form of a look from a stranger on the street, or a driver who doesn't like the way we drive. Sometimes we get more direct feedback, like in a job review. Sometimes it is great, but once in a while we get feedback that really hurts.

I received some feedback from someone whose opinion I valued. They had given a similar message before, but this time the method of delivering it had changed, and it struck me like a hammer. That conversation triggered something in me that I knew needed to heal. It had me questioning what I believed and what I felt about who I was. While such events had in the past been nonproductive in helping me heal, this one peeled back the illusions that were on my map of reality.

We all love Rocky, the rags to riches story of a boxer, because he gets up after being knocked down and no matter what someone throws at him, he gets up again. I wonder if we would like him or his story as much if one of the hits took him down and he did not rise again. This time I had trouble rising up.

I wondered, for a time, what difference it would make in the world if I didn't rise again.

I eventually got back on my feet, ready to fight another day, but I have to ask myself why I let someone else's opinion take me down. When we fall short of another's expectations, what is an appropriate response?

Getting feedback potentially puts us into transition. We can choose to accept and incorporate it, if the feedback has value, or we can let it go if it does not fit who we are. Or there is a third choice - take what has value and let the rest go.

I have come to the conclusion that the ego is very sneaky.

My perception of life was shifting under my feet again, and while I didn't like the feelings that it brought up in me, I welcomed the change. Each time I allowed myself to feel and become aware of what was being brought up in my interactions with others, I learned who I was on a deeper level. Realizing and embracing the only constant in my life which has been change helped to make the journey easier.

Words, for me, have always been part of the way I feel loved. I'm not speaking literally about the overused phrase "I love you", but words spoken from the heart hold enormous weight for me. I often wonder why that is. Words like honor, truth, justice, and freedom, speak to my soul.

My favorite speech in the movie *Independence Day* is where the president says, "We will not go quietly into the night. We're going to live on. We're going to survive. Today we celebrate our Independence Day!" It stirs feelings of hope in me.

So what does this all mean? I wish I could tie it up in a nice, succinct sentence, but for now I will leave it open. Words have a power all of their own to stir, empower, and fill the hearts of the people we meet every day. Words can fill us with empowering beliefs or tear us down.

Sometimes our purpose is found through simple things. My love of words and desire to be a champion for "Truth" and "Justice" helped me make sense of my purpose. All we need is for the intention to be set and to have faith that the future is coming. My intention is to remove all the non-resourceful thoughts and beliefs that are on my map of reality so I can be part of the solution.

In the past, I had often found myself working on what I didn't want. Thoughts like "I just don't want to suck!" I" don't want to be alone.", "I don't want you to do x or y or z.", "I don't want to be broke." or "I don't want to be fat." I always justified it by thinking I would finish that and then sometime in the undefined future I could work on have what I did want. I looked at it almost like paying my dues, but I did this until I was no longer in touch with what I wanted. I did what I thought was expected of me, believing that others knew better than me. I was most comfortable going with the flow. I did not have a strong enough desire to fight for what I thought I wanted.

Jim Carrey, the actor, says it well, "When working on something you don't want, you can still fail, so why not work on something you do want?"

I hadn't reflected very much on what success meant to me. In hindsight, I worked largely off the theory that I was just struggling to survive and trying to be good enough for others to want me in business, in my personal life, etc. I was not content with anything I did because I feared not being able to repeat it.

Any marketing campaign I created and won awards for were flukes. Getting a top award from the Authentic Speaker Academy for Leadership was a mistake. I feared that the successful SEO campaigns I did for companies were going to fail sometime in the undefined future. Even a cake I made was not good enough because it was probably not level or didn't look right.

What had I done to myself over those years? Writing the previous paragraph brought tears to my eyes for the woman that I was then. Where in your life are you judging yourself so harshly that the pleasure of a job well done eludes you? Do you need to rethink your definition of success?

When speaking about goals it is easy to get into the mindset of *all or nothing*. Either we made it or we didn't, and we forget the successes along the way. It is easy to become discouraged if our vision or goal is big. Often we measure our progress by how close the goal is. This is like deciding to walk to the horizon. If you get up tomorrow and start walking, how close will you be to the horizon by nightfall? It will seem just as far away. If instead, you measure by where you started, you can see the progress you made during your journey. By celebrating all the little steps or successes along the way, we become present to our life and become happier along the way.

Takeaway:

When we, as women, begin the journey to awaken our inner power the way might not be clear. Perhaps we only know what we don't want and not necessarily what we do want. But by taking the first step forward, we set the intention and direction. This allows the future you want, room to come into your life. Work toward what you want, not what you don't want. Recognize your successes along the way and the way will get easier and not seem so overwhelming.

Stepping Stones:

Where in your life are you judging yourself so harshly that the pleasure of a job well done is eluding you?

_____

_____

_____

_____

_____

_____

_____

VICTORIA HARGIS

_____

_____

_____

_____

_____

_____

_____

_____

_____

_____

_____

_____

_____

_____

What does success look like to you?

_____

_____

_____

_____

_____

_____

_____

_____

_____

_____

_____

_____

_____

Start a success journal. Write 100 successes that you have had and remember to give yourself a break. Small successes count as much as big ones. Some days, just getting out of bed is a success.

_____

_____

_____

_____

_____

_____

_____

_____

_____

_____

_____

_____

_____

VICTORIA HARGIS

_____

_____

_____

_____

_____

_____

_____

_____

_____

_____

_____

_____

_____

_____

_____

_____

_____

_____

_____

_____

_____

_____

_____

_____

_____

_____

_____

_____

CHAPTER 5

It's Not Pretty

Clean Out the C.R.A.P.

Growth is not pretty. I am not sure that I ever had the ability to get through life with elegance, ease, and grace... at least so far. And I am not sure that it matters how I grow, as long as I am growing. Cleaning out the C.R.A.P means we are willing to get rid of the mental clutter that is holding us stuck. In order to allow what we want into our life we need to let go of the conflicts, resentments, attitudes and procrastinations or problems that you are still carrying with you from the past.

When you go within yourself to connect to your purpose, it will not be easy to face all the emotions that get stirred up. You will be confronted again with all the emotions that you may have been told, in the past, were not acceptable. You will begin to experience them all over again so that you can process them and heal. I was extremely alarmed and upset when I realized that I had to feel all those emotions again. I hadn't even wanted to feel them the first time! I learned, after starting my journey, that if the feelings are not dealt with, they will run my life by self-sabotage and I will find myself back in the same situations over and over again. So I determined I would clean out all the conflicts, resentments, attitudes and problems or procrastinations that came up as I live my life.

There had been a rage inside me that bubbled up periodically over the years. I could conquer it each time and quiet it for a while, but it seemed unrelenting and almost uncontrollable to me. It would scare me when I was younger because it seemed so big. I know now it was my soul screaming for change. I can now trust myself to feel that deeply and not lose control. It is good and necessary to feel. In my childhood, rage was beaten down until there was no feeling.

I can still see little Victoria all alone and looking lost. Her rage was my rage and yet I had not held her or comforted her. I left her feeling alone, as though I did not have the power to protect her in this world.

I camouflaged that rage in niceness, conforming to what I felt I was supposed to do as a woman, wife, widow, mother, and grandmother. In that conformity there is a sense of safety, as if following everyone else's wishes would guarantee no pain.

My karate instructor once said I have an indomitable spirit. I liked that thought. I think back over my life and I know that my spirit rose up and carried me through everything that life had to offer as I struggled to conform.

Now I've learned how to be, as the self-destructive rage dies off and the soft tender insides start peeking through. Phrases as simple as "I love you" or "I believe in you" melted away my sense of pain. The rage had kept me from collapsing under the heavy pain of my history, it served a purpose previously. That rage would not let me quit when everything seemed hopeless, but I no longer need the rage that kept me alive all those years.

I read the words "toxic shame" in a book by John Bradshaw on healing the inner child. I thought I understood what he meant until I came face to face with my inner two-year-old and saw the guilt that she had felt for just being alive. I never realized what a burden I had put on her.

Even as I wrote those words I felt the tears come to my eyes. Each of these realizations has truly been bought at a great price. I'm not one who can cry easily, even over things I feel strongly about, but each tear brings a little bit more release and a little bit more clarity about who I am.

As humans, we have an innate need to connect and belong to a tribe. When that human need is not met in a positive way, we experience shame and feel rejection. This shame is toxic and becomes engrained. When yearnings to belong are ignored, dismissed, rejected, or when we are shamed, criticized, judged, or humiliated for those longings on a regular basis, it changes our world view.

Much like being smashed against the wall had created a point which marked me until I faced it years later, we need to face the shame that we may have felt for being alive. Until that happens, we shut down the part of us that wants to connect.

As Linda Graham tells us in *Bouncing Back: Rewiring Your Brain for Maximum Resilience and Well-Being*[4], when toxic shame occurs, *"Our activation to reach out and engage immediately contracts; we withdraw, shut down, and hide. Our yearnings are paired with pain, literally heartache or heartbreak. Toxic shame curls the once hopeful – now wounded – children inside, up into a ball of pain and hurt, hiding in defensive, isolating caves, protecting themselves as best they can against further rejection and humiliation."*

I've gone through many stages searching for my inner child. There were many times in my past where things happened to me that caused me to compartmentalize parts of myself into different boxes. At times I felt like I was living with holes perforated through my soul and my spirit. I navigated around those holes and I lived my life to the best of my ability, but I always felt sharp edges or empty holes where I was trying to force myself to be what I was *supposed* to be. I have wondered many times who I would have been in different circumstances.

But I was who I was, and I did live every one of those years. Every one of my inner children splintered away until I felt there was not much of me left. Yet I married, raised my kids, became a widow, and led a mission to heal my youngest son. When that ended, I was left wondering what to do with my life. I walked

---

4 Graham, Linda. *Bouncing Back: Rewiring Your Brain for Maximum Resilience and Well-being*. N.p.: n.p., n.d. Print.

on distant shores from where I was raised and wondered sometimes what a weird sense of humor God has. A victim should
not feel shame yet that is what I felt during those times when
someone might have mistaken me for a victim.

I chose this life; all of it;
Choosing what I wanted to learn;
Before, I came bright-eyed
and so very weak as an infant
I don't remember why I chose it,
But I know it was an important reason.

So I refused to see myself as a victim
Rising each time determined
To learn from each event
What it was I was to learn.
Being the victim gave me many things,
Empathy and an understanding of so much of life
And the human condition.

So I understand what motivates Victims
How to avoid antagonizing the abuser.
How to walk on eggshells
And other assorted stuffs.

And I had to choose what I would be
Instead of blindly choosing what was
Because what was,
Was intolerable for my spirit
Which is why I chose differently
As much as I could

I'm not quite sure how this all comes together with
My life's purpose,
But I know, as sure as I know I chose this Life,
That it does

I would not trade any of my experiences away
Because they brought me to this place and this time.
With my spirit rejoicing and loving and being.

We women have the capacity to change the world. Not until we hit the turning point where we decide no more, do we begin our journey to discover our purpose on this earth.

Once we awaken, we are like the mommabear, ferocious and unwilling to accept anything less than what is right in any given situation.

In order to become a leader, you need to clean out the crap, conflict, resentments, attitudes, and procrastinations. Those that you choose to hang on to are what is preventing you from stepping into your new life.

Takeaway:

I tell you this story to let you know that no matter how hard it is or how big the obstacle, if you have a clear purpose, that is what matters. Choose to get up when knocked down because "Hard does not matter... purpose does." If you can't remember your purpose, or if it temporarily seems to be gone, then remember that you had it once.

Get up and fight again until it becomes clear. Then write your purpose in big capital letters that you emotionally connect with and post it where you see it every day.

Stepping Stones:

How many times a day do you find yourself blocked by real or imagined obstacles?

_____

_____

_____

_____

_____

_____

Take one simple little step toward your future. You don't have to climb the mountain in one day.

Each step counts.

What simple step can you take right now that will bring you one step closer to your dream?

_____

_____

_____

_____

_____

_____

CHAPTER 6

Hiding in Plain Sight

Accept Failure as the Fastest Way to Success

We are responsible for our own choices and we choose what occurs in our lives. Sometimes those choices are subconscious. When we can get to the point where we take total responsibility for what shows up in our life, we gain back our power. One way to look at this is, if you operate as one who does not have control over the events in your life, then you are like a leaf being tossed around by the wind. Being at the mercy of someone else's whim can make life seem pretty dismal. If instead you take control and make decisions based on how your choices manifest in your life, then you can make adjustments to create the life you want. If you did not produce the result you wanted, simply choose something different next time.

Sometimes I had to hide because it felt like I was bombarded with the emotions of everyone around me. That was letting life happen to me and not choosing what I wanted. Once I chose who and what I would let affect me, I could then decide what my life would be.

> *"The individual has always had to struggle to keep from being overwhelmed by the tribe. If you try it, you will be lonely often, and sometimes frightened, but no price is too high to pay for the privilege of owning yourself."* —Friedrich Nietzsche

I have failed many times in my life. These failures are important steps on the journey within. Until I was willing to fail, I stayed stuck in the world I knew, separated from the world I wanted.

I often wondered why I had such conflict over belonging to groups. In the past, if I joined a group, it seemed that the group disbanded within a few short months or years. I often felt as if there was something in me that caused the group to fall apart. I avoided joining groups for years because when the groups imploded it was so painful. I was lonely, but I also survived quite well by myself.

Eventually I joined another group, one whose goal was authenticity. This group also imploded, but it was different this time, because I had grown to the point where I was able to assert boundaries. I was relieved to find that the eventual implosion did not affect me like it would have in the past. I had grown.

I have been telling the story of my decision to become a speaker in my talks lately. I got the idea when I was attending the 2007 Figure Business Seminar on Long Island put on by a famous internet marketer. A speaker had just left the stage and I turned to my companion and said, "I want to do that someday: be able to speak on the stage." There was only one slight problem... I was afraid of even saying my name in front of a group.

Much later, in 2010, I attended a weeklong business retreat in Texas. It was a hot summer night with a thousand stars lighting up the night sky. We gathered in silence in the lobby of the lodge for the last night of the week. Single file, we walked silently, hearing the beat of a drum echo in time to the footfalls on the path.

We gathered on the blankets, spread on the ground to remove our shoes and socks, and prepared to walk on hot coals, 850 degrees, twenty foot fire walk. We were instructed that we would need to stand at the head of the fire and state what hurdle we were trying to break through and what goal we were walking toward, prior to commencing the fire walk.

I sweated and panicked as I waited for my turn. The only thought in my head was "I have to say two sentences in front of the group. What if I do it wrong?" I must have practiced those two sentences fifty times while I sat waiting.

When it was my turn, my heart pounded in fear. I walked to the start. I was so nervous that I'm not quite sure what I said before I began to walk, placing my feet carefully on the bed of hot coals. At ten feet in, the half way mark, I hit my watershed mommabear moment. All past failures to speak seemed to meet my future years and I simply decided I would not live like that anymore.

I came home, joined Toastmasters, and set a goal to give one speech per month. I gave speech after speech until I got my Competent Communicator Award and then my Competent Leadership Award, both within the first year and a half. The fear of speaking in public was conquered, but I was not content because I still feared speaking on an international stage. So I set a new goal: I applied for, and got accepted to, The Authentic Speaker Academy for Leadership.

At the academy, the odds were stacked against me. At that point, I had been shut down emotionally following the death of my son to such a degree, that the question of how I could be authentic was a serious question. And the next issue of how to present in a way that was engaging seemed like even more of a long shot.

It literally took me months to be able to smile in the homework videos. I got really tired of being told I looked like a *"deer in the headlights"*. The mere thought of trying to be humorous had me twisted in knots. After months of trying, the only accent I could come up with was Southern, and I could not even hold it for a complete sentence. Practicing VAK (speaking in different modalities of Visual, Auditory and Kinesthetic) felt like a foreign battlefield. I created spreadsheets for daily work that I needed to practice. Accents, VAK, professional voice training, dressing makeovers, and practicing sexy walks to get movement back into my body were just some of what I studied. I even danced weekly via Skype with a coach so I could reclaim my body's natural comfort in moving.

The signature story that formed the basis of my presentation changed three times over the course of six months. The day before the final boot camp, I questioned everything I was doing because the mountain seemed so high and I felt so incapable of climbing it. I knew that there were people that thought I did not belong and thought I would not make it, but this just made me more determined. I would at least go down fighting. Some of my family thought I was making things up as I told my life story. I had business associates that questioned what I was sharing.

I persevered through it all. I was not sure until the week before the graduation symposium that I would make it onto the stage. As I spoke the night of graduation, to a crowd of over 100 people, I felt connected to each and every one of them. I shared my life story about finding and living my purpose.

At the end of the evening, I was honored with the 2013 President's Excellence Award for consistently demonstrating outstanding leadership qualities.

I spent years, not claiming leadership qualities that I had earned honestly from having lived the story. My expertise is in what I have done and my strength is in what I am willing to do. I am a leader in my own life and in the lives of the people I touch.

Where in your life are you not claiming and owning who you are?

Women leaders have fascinating differences from men leaders. It is a touchy concept to point out, but it has certainly been my experience. The mommabear comes out so easily when we women find something to be passionate about. Until that happens, we seem to be largely content to live our lives on the passive side, preferring to let things be.

Is it in a misguided attempt to protect the people around us from the discomfort of change? Where does that come from? How many of us came from homes where the primary message was that we were to wait for Prince Charming to come so that we could live happily ever after?

We learn early on that there is safety in hiding who we are. Many of us hid for years in plain sight as we became wives and mothers and quietly raised our kids. We also have hidden our-selves in corporations by sitting back and not playing bigger.

I can feel the words waiting
Like an unexplored bomb
Unstable waiting for just the
Unintended spark that will set off
The untended dynamite carelessly
Left to sit

Words that are held by iron bars
That strangle my heart
That felt wrong to speak
Kept silent in order to not feel
The stings and arrows that would
Pierce my soul

I silence myself in face of
Maleness believing that

That is the normal and that I must
Not stretch beyond my place, my station
And to do so is arrogance
Of an untutored Feminine Soul
Who is so broken
She does not understand her place.

And yet
it is the words that will also free me
Expressing and making sense of
My world and my place
Which is no place and every place
And so I speak not ever to hurt or maim,
but in a final cry that I must live
I choose to live, to live abundantly

What a burden that is, for the men in our lives to be made to feel responsible for our happiness. If we are not happy, don't we have to take responsibility for the choices we make?

Otherwise our world remains small and we don't take on any more responsibilities than an inanimate, porcelain doll that never grows.

When I was young girl I did not fit in because I had no desire to be a porcelain doll. I liked trucks, cowboys, Indians, and figuring out how things go together. As I went to school, I saw how girls stood on the sidelines and cheered on the boys who got to play. I never liked that and always felt like the odd one out just because I wanted to play too.

That feeling persisted over the years, even after I started my own company. I made money every year, but not the kind of money I wanted to make. I was not playing on a bigger field.

I was still held back by my conditioned beliefs that women are supposed to be passive and not want to play in the big leagues. There was a continual inner tug of war where I held myself back because I was not supposed to want the things I wanted.

This frustration led to a period of time where I was depressed. I don't believe in drugging myself with prescription drugs, especially when the response is not just chemical, but a genuine reaction to a real problem. I still felt paralyzed and unable get motivated to do anything. I was finally moved to get off the couch and do karate to support my oldest grandson. I didn't want to do it, but I forced myself to go one day a week. I can't say that was enough to change anything huge in my life, but it did begin to shift things a little.

The sun burst through
Almost blinding me by its brilliance
Cutting through the heaviness
That surrounds me
Has surrounded me drowning me
Stifling the words that can free
My words that are becoming unfrozen
Warmed by the simple shaft of light
Can it be so simple to speak what is in my heart
A simple beam of light shone into the frozen expanse
Of unspoken words can unlock the tortured words

Until I speak freely not practiced but what is in my heart
That will connect me to the world and my soul at once
One; at the same time one to the many
Connected, so connected to those who love and listen
To the words that come so slowly, slowly thawing
From my heart

Instrumental to the watershed moment of my mommabear coming out of hibernation, was the weeklong retreat in Texas. Walking that fire walk became the line in the sand where I decided no more! I would define myself from then on and I would define what my life would become.

I believe there comes a point in every woman's life where she wakes the mommabear up and becomes the leader that will make a difference in her own life and in the lives of the women around her.

Takeaway:

Leaders know that there comes a time to step forward with faith. Even if everything in you is saying it's not possible, you need to force yourself to do it anyway. Realize that refusing to make a choice in your life is still making a choice. Even the worst day can still be a day where you choose to be happy.

Stepping Stones:

What is your life worth? If I asked right now what your life was worth, what would you say?

_____

_____

_____

_____

_____

_____

_____

_____

_____

_____

What are you willing to give up in order to spend time working on what your heart wants?

_____

_____

_____

_____

_____

What fills you with indignation?

_____

_____

_____

_____

_____

_____

How do you need to heal your heart going forward?

_____

_____

_____

_____

_____

_____

CHAPTER 7

Fighting on the Side of Angels

Live with Honor

Davey would come home from school and immediately recommence fighting the epic internal battles that are part of our world. Not many people openly speak about the difficulty of the human condition. Even less addressed is the special difficulty for children in facing the confusing inner demons of anger and frustration over who we are and what is happening to us in this world.

Anger is not necessarily a good or bad emotion. It is just a response to fear over what is taking place in our environment. We all experience anger. Sometimes we mask it with other things like alcohol, food, or shopping.

We can use anger as a tool to help us make sense of our realities and uncover our convictions. Otherwise anger is just a projection of something we fear inside. It can happen instinctively when we defend our positions about sensitive subjects. This is a great learning opportunity since it can be a clear signal telling us when there is something we need to look at in order to continue to grow.

I had often quieted my own hidden anger in a less obvious way. What I did was perhaps more socially acceptable, but no less deadening to my soul. I covered my anger in Big Gulps from 7-11, candy, and mind-numbing entertainment to get through the day.

In truth, my anger scared me. It reminded me of the anger that was so vehemently expressed in my house as I grew up. It is true that anger can destroy things and tear us down, but there is also a righteous anger that can push us forward. It can provide rocket fuel to galvanize us into action to right a wrong or make huge changes in our lives.

Anger has always seemed so risky that I avoided it at all costs. Always deflecting hurts or violations of my boundaries by justifying that the perpetrator did not know what they were doing. I reassured myself that I knew better, so I could simply overlook wrongs. What a bunch of hogwash! All I was doing was denying myself and ignoring my desires in an effort to feel safe and avoid confrontation.

For me, anger was the acknowledgement of all the places that felt trashed inside of me. It took time to work through the devastations of my life. It is important to note that feeling the anger, or any emotion, is not the same as throwing a temper tantrum or lashing out at another person. Anger is just an emotion, to be distinguished from the actual action or angry behavior.

Many times anger is a sign that something is not right. Sometimes anger is guilt turned outward. When you do things to serve the anger, you can get stuck. I had the opposite problem. I had a very hard time feeling and acknowledging the anger to begin with, so anger in me expressed itself as shame.

I wish I could be as clear as Davey was, fighting on the side of the angels and always having an unwavering vision of right and wrong.

I had struggled throughout the years to stay true to myself and own my journey. I consciously worked to remove the distorted lens through which I had seen the world, to try to see reality more objectively.

It is rare to get a clear view of what is really happening in any situation. Most often our views are so colored by the lens of our conditioned beliefs that no two people can recall the same event identically. That is why it seems so easy to be in disagreement with someone. To reach a consensus with another, both must be willing to examine their own conditioned beliefs.

I wonder sometimes what Davey saw and knew, and whether he saw things more clearly than I did then and do now. I believe children are closer to the divine. They seem to instinctively see more clearly and to know what is right in situations.

One inspiring group of children from a tribe in Africa believes that the idea of one person winning while others lose is unthinkable. An anthropologist had brought treats and candy to this tribe that he had been studying. On the last day, he placed all the remaining treats in a basket under a tree then drew a line in the dirt a little distance from the basket.

He had the children line up and asked them race to the tree.

He told them the first to arrive would get all the candy. When he said go, they simply joined hands and ran to the tree as a group.

Once there, they shared the candy with each other and happily ate it. The anthropologist was very surprised. He asked them why they had all gone together, especially if the first one to arrive at the tree could have won everything in the basket - all the sweets. A young girl simply replied: "How can one of us be happy if all the others are sad?" Perhaps it is we who do not see clearly, with our constant jockeying for position, material wealth, and status.

"Africans have a thing called ubuntu. It is about the essence of being human, it is part of the gift that Africa will give the world. It embraces hospitality, caring about others, being willing to go the extra mile for the sake of another. We believe that a person is a person through other persons, that my humanity is caught up, bound up, inextricably with yours. When I dehumanize you, I inexorably dehumanize myself. The solitary human being is a contradiction in terms. Therefore you seek to work for the common good because your

humanity comes into its own in community, in belonging."
—Archbishop Desmond Tutu

It can be very challenging to make any changes in our life's direction, but there are a number of things we can do to either accelerate the changes or to short circuit our growth. We are masters of sabotaging our progress. We second guess ourselves. We hear over and over again about what we are not doing right. Whether it is raising our kids, being acceptable socially, or even whether we are grieving correctly.

As long as you are moving in the direction your heart tells you, then you cannot be doing it wrong. The heart is an accurate compass to reassure you that wherever you go next is exactly where you needed to go at the time.

It is an old paradigm to view great leaders as inspiring and pushing underlings to create something great. There are many conflicting books and articles written about what makes a great leader.

I believe it all comes down to being real and owning your own power. The only way to do that is to spend time going within so that you can operate from a place of authenticity. Authenticity is not a static place. A person can only operate authentically from the place where they currently are. This is a journey that will never end. You can always go deeper and know yourself better. It takes a strong leader to do the hard work of going within and fighting the personal demons in order to reclaim themselves from conditioned beliefs.

To be a real leader means that you must always be willing to examine places where you are not operating from your highest self in any given situation. You are willing to be fully present and available to others on your team. You welcome their input and realize that we are all co-creating the realities we are living. This is true whether it is the success of a company or the relationships we have with one another.

Part of my own self-examination process led me to read *Women's Reality* by Anne Wilson Schaef.[5] It is a truly powerful book that clearly spells out some of the systems in play in our world.

I had always been able to sense the unspoken rules that seemed to contradict what was said or spoken aloud and which made for a very confusing world view. Schaef's book gave me a perspective and the words to be able to understand why I was able to sense the underlying power dynamics inside of a group.

In her book, Schaef describes the White Male System as defensive of the status quo. It can feel fearful living in a paradigm of power that sometimes comes across as asserting a "my way or the highway" negotiation approach with those who are less privileged. As a woman growing up and living in this kind of environment, I struggled to adapt to and gain the approval of this culture. I felt that it discounted my unique perceptions and talents while insisting that I conform to limited, stereotyped roles.

---

5 Schaef, Anne Wilson. *Women's Reality: An Emerging Female System in the White Male Society.* Minneapolis, MN: Winston, 1981. Print.

In Schaef's book, the White Male System seems to view responsibility punitively and as a method of targeting blame - as in "The buck stops here!" In her Female System, responsibility is expressed as the willingness and ability to respond.

Exercising leadership by using your muscles of persuasion, trust, respect, and relationships is far more difficult than command and control style; however, the payoffs are greater because we go from a bureaucracy to being driven by values and a shared purpose.

Traditionally, being a leader meant that you made the decisions for a group and then delegated to the group what they needed to do to accomplish the goal that you had already previously decided. Research seems to suggest that this leadership model is not as effective as it used to be.
It appears that we have shifted to another stage of evolution in corporate structure.

At the current rate of attrition, seventy-five percent of the S&P 500 will be replaced by 2027. Currently a company only lasts eighteen years on the index, compared to sixty-one years in 1958. Perhaps the old ways of being a leader are not serving companies well in the long run and we can enter a new era of business.

A study by the National Bureau of Economic Research suggests that decisions made by groups are, on the average, better than those made by individuals. But any group is still vulnerable to defaulting to a top-down hierarchy and suffering from the constraints of "group think".

RAW LEADERSHIP

What purpose does it serve to live in a country of healthy and profitable companies if they slowly erode the quality of life of the communities they serve and the lives of its employees?

Work should be a means to a quality life not the main part of one's life.

Power over vs Power with
What is it about hierarchy
That saddens my heart
So much that it feels
Like it is breaking

I get that having structure
Helps move things around
And sometimes even forward
If not backward.
Maybe it is not
Hierarchy
Maybe that thought is incorrect

Hierarchy
That I have blamed for the
Pain that I have seen in my life
Repressed lost souls playing
A game of it really matters
With as much passion as they
Can muster in between drinks
At the bar and well thought out
Position statements

I wonder if they realize how little
It really matters
Maybe it is the lack of personal
Leadership

We are already in the midst of substantial change. The millennials that are entering the workforce don't accept old paradigms. If the corporation does not fit their values and purpose, then they are willing to leave at an ever-increasing rate. They believe in mission over money and don't seem to be tied to working in a certain place. They operate largely with the belief that judgment trumps rules.

If companies can transform the way they operate to match the way these new workers think, they will reap the rewards. The world is changing either way.

We can embrace the change and step into the new world fully engaged with our purpose, or we can get relegated to the sidelines.

This shift in the paradigm of leadership works to women's advantage since we are typically less attached or pressured to identify ourselves as the main leader. Think of a family gathering where every woman brings or creates something to help the party along. Even those of us who are cooking-challenged stop by the store to bring something to help the meal.

"We can't help but wonder how much difference one person makes in the world. We look inside ourselves, questioning

if we have the capacity for heroism and greatness, but the truth is every time we take an action, we make an impact. Every single thing we do has an effect on the people around us. Every choice we make sends ripples out into the world. Our smallest acts of kindness can cause a chain reaction of unforeseen benefits for people we've never met. We might not witness those results, but they happen all the same."[6]
—Jake Bohm, *Touch*

Each of us has an impact in this world. The question is: what affect are you having? Are you creating more light or more darkness in this world? Are you part of the solution or part of the problem?

Takeaway:

Leaders seeing clearly, and being willing to fight on the side of angels, gladdens your inner being. The first step to seeing clearly is to embrace both the darkness and light within so you can free yourself from your conditioned beliefs.

All the emotions you feel are signposts on your path to help you free yourself and move through them. Experience them, but don't get stuck. Continue on the path to inner freedom.

---

6 *Tim Kring, screenwriter, Touch TV Series 2012-2013*

Stepping Stones:

Think of a particularly challenging situation that made you angry and ask yourself:

Why am I reacting with anger to this situation?

_____

_____

_____

_____

_____

Are you residing in anger more than in happiness?

_____

_____

_____

_____

_____

What is your primary response to things? Are you negative, positive, or neutral by default?

_____

_____

_____

_____

_____

_____

Do the people in your life view you as positive or negative?

_____

_____

_____

_____

_____

What are you consistently avoiding in your life?

_____

_____

_____

_____

_____

_____

Where in your life do you know you're playing small?

_____

_____

_____

_____

_____

_____

CHAPTER 8

A Matter of Perspective

Be Ferocious In Discovering Your Truth

We all like to think that we own the truth. If everyone else just thought like we do, or acted like we do, then the world would be a better place, right? We like to think that the way we were raised is the right way and that it is the only way to live. That gets us into trouble when we place those expectations on other people and they do not respond as we expected.

The thought that any one person has a monopoly on the truth is an egomaniacal way to think. Unfortunately, we see this in some religions and in many politicians. The temptation to demonize those who are different and raise the "righteous" onto a pedestal may happen because it is a cheap way of gaining a following. It is unfortunate that the pedestal is so narrow because the righteous are continually falling off of it.

We have to root out our own conditioned beliefs and search for the truth hidden within the rules and structures of our lives. We lead small lives and get angry over small things.

Somewhere in all of that we lose our larger selves. We cannot find truths by refusing to look at reality. We need to ask whether our current roadmap is bringing us closer to or farther from where we want to be.

I believe that the real original sin is the desire to control another person. The bible says, "You hypocrite, first cast out the beam from your own eye; and then shall you see clearly to cast out the speck from your brother's eye." How much pain and anguish has been caused by the desire to fix or control another?

A far better use of time and resources is to fix YOU.

The idea that by healing ourselves, we actually heal the world, has been gaining in popularity in recent years. It's a way of living that is clearly a far better use of energy and resources. We can consistently control what we do, whereas we can rarely maintain any control over another's actions.

When my children, Davey and Doug, were fighting about the music each listened to, Davey would call Doug's music devil music. The argument seemed to be a never-ending discussion or should I say fight. In reality, the music was Bon Jovi, Metallica, etc. Davey could not see Doug's point of view and Doug could not see Davey's point of view. And so the fight went on.

I have seen this rigidity played out in politics, family gatherings, discussion groups, on Facebook, and on other social media. Even asking questions can be seen as an attack and could get you unfriended.

What if we walked in another person's shoes for a while and tried to see things from their perspective? What insights would we gain? What new ways of seeing things might occur? What new solutions to problems could we add into our repertoire?

We can only operate from within the limitations of our own internal map of reality, but what if the map is too limited to see all the possibilities that lie further out? What if there is someone in our life that has a larger map of reality with more options?

What if the person we are vehemently attacking is the person whose map is more effective? What would it hurt to actively listen with an open heart to what they have to say?

When Galileo postulated that the earth was not the center of the universe, he was vehemently denounced, ostracized, and eventually excommunicated from the Roman Catholic Church. He spent the rest of his life under house arrest. We now know that Galileo was correct, but think of the energy and effort that went toward proving him wrong.

What would happen if, instead of trying to prove the other person wrong, we tried to hear what they were saying? Looking to see things from another's point of view can give us insight into the problems that face this world. It is rarely, if ever, true that one side is completely right on all points and the other side completely wrong on all points.

The next time you find yourself in conflict with someone, try this method of expanding your perspective. Start by naming the different perspectives of the problem or conflict. Take index cards and write a different perspective on each card.

Place the cards on the floor, take a breath, and slowly breathe out to ground yourself and remain in the present.

Step onto one of the cards and enter that perspective. Talk about the problem from that perspective without judging how that perspective sees things.

When you have exhausted that perspective, step off the card, take a breath, and reground yourself. Step onto the next card and repeat the process with the new perspective. Most importantly, remember to do this without judgment.

It didn't seem quite fair that the search for meaning in my life was so convoluted. I searched in all the usual places to find the fulfillment that had eluded me over the years. I searched in my religion, family, and social groups, thinking that what I was missing inside was out there. The idea that it could actually be inside me was unthinkable to me.

The death of Davey, after working so hard to get him well, was the catalyst that cracked me wide open to begin a journey of self-discovery. This journey was solitary and very lonely. Only in the course of shattering my being was I able to find the spark inside of me that had refused to die in the long, dull winter of my life. That spark called to me to start, try, and begin again.

There were no promises of success, there never is when beginning such a journey. There were countless rocks, hurdles, quicksand, and canyons that stood between me and eventual success. This was an epic journey. Not a hero's journey, but a heroine's journey. I was not slaying dragons, but gathering the parts of me that had been discarded or beaten out of me, and it was truly a battle.

Each of these parts fit together to create the mosaic of my life. It has been a grand journey, even if some of it involved me crawling inch by inch, refusing to give up, until I reached the treasure. The treasure was and is my essential self. Reaching the "me" that I was supposed to be before life happened was the prize. I saved myself.

The journey wades through the swamps of all the "shoulds" and "have tos" and the shaming and distractions of physical violence that made "just being" more difficult. Men, although often less vulnerable to being dominated, don't have it any easier on their epic journey. The journey and the way we go about it is just different. Maybe what we think we are seeking is different.

"The main difference between the hero and the heroine's journey," popular illustrator, Alice Meichi Li says, *"is when a hero is striving to become a master, a heroine is striving for equality and normality."* Li says a brief summation of Joseph Campbell's *Hero's Journey* would be *"A boy's coming*

of age where the student becomes the master. That would be the most basic." About female leading roles, Li says instead: *"A heroine is thrust into a world gone mad. Everything has flipped and turned upside down and heroines are struggling to find their way home. They feel that they are the only sane ones."*[7]

The key to the heroine's journey is not her reward for victory, but how and why she fights, struggles, and perseveres to the end. In other words, the moral is how well she journeys, not what she wins in the end.

It seems as if, to a woman, who she becomes is more important than the outcome of the situation. The process trumps the potential victory. The victory is in playing the game as herself and not in defeating the enemy. It is a more centered way of looking at life

The heroine struggles to be herself even in the midst of total chaos.

How I perceive me is not how the world perceives me. Some in the world saw me as an inspiration, yet when I was going through the journey with Davey, I saw myself as a failure. Practicing self-love would have allowed me the eyes to see what others saw.

---

7 Franklin, Nicole. "The Hero's Journey vs. The Heroine's Journey: Rewriting Privilege -." *The Good Men Project*. N.p., 07 Dec. 2014. Web. 14 Apr. 2016.

Takeaway:

Leaders know that there are many shades of gray in any situation. No one is all right and no one is all wrong. She is willing to look at all sides and discern the truth of situations. She learned to do this when mediating between the children she loves and helping them heal.

A leader recognizes and teaches those around her how to see the situation from all sides. No one owns the truth. Learn to appreciate what others have to teach us.

Stepping Stones:

What environment in your life do you need to declutter to have space for what you want in your life?

_____

_____

_____

_____

_____

_____

_____

Remember that clutter is not necessarily physical.

Are there parts of yourself that you are refusing to see as you really are?

_____

_____

_____

_____

_____

_____

_____

_____

_____

_____

What blinders are you wearing that prevent you from seeing the truth?

_____

_____

_____

_____

_____

_____

_____

_____

_____

_____

_____

_____

CHAPTER 9

I Like the Statue with the Penis

Embrace Humor and Joy

One day Davey and I went to the art museum as a reward for working the program. We used poker chips as a currency and he earned enough chips through the Social Code of Excellence to go on the outing. While we were there and walking through the Impressionist gallery, Davey pointed out a Degas correctly, even though he had never been shown that particular piece of art as part of his program.

It was small signs like this along the way that kept me going. By showing Davey a set of ten paintings by Edgar Degas, he was able to correctly identify the artist's work by his style. I could see his intelligence growing; it was almost like the pathways in his brain were being formed right before my eyes.

Later, after we got home, Davey wrote a letter to the doctor at The Institutes about his experience at the museum.

Dear Ann Ball,

I went to the art museum
My Favorite is the
Naked Man with a penis
I ate dinner

Love Davey

I liked the fact that he was learning so well. Davey liked the naked man with a penis sculpture. It was a win-win.

Sometimes humor is the only way to survive what can be the craziness of life. When I was enrolled in the Authentic Speaker Academy for Leadership, we had assignments that required us to create a video and upload it to YouTube every week. I looked like a talking head in the videos and struggled with the feedback each week as the reviews came in.

The particular moniker that I had been given was "deer in the headlights". Big eyes, motionless body, looking ready to be run over: that was me. It was very frustrating. I had no clue how to not look like that, and all my attempts to smile seemed to fail. I would do one take after another, all in an attempt to get past this particular image.

One afternoon I was attempting to create a two-minute video explaining the leadership principle "Failure is an Important Ingredient in My Success, Quitting is Not". I did take after take, and in each video I was exactly the same; the deer was still present. On take number forty-six, I began screaming and stomping around. I hit the wall in my frustration.

All of a sudden, I began laughing at the fact that I was throwing a temper tantrum because I felt I was failing. Failure was exactly what the video was about. That broke the log jam and I shot the video on the very next take. The reviews came back saying the "deer had migrated north". Sometimes when we remember to laugh, we relax enough to actually accomplish what we wanted.

I was the proverbial lost child, being the middle kid. I was rejected by my parents at birth and it was hard to be seen in my large family. Part of my journey has been accepting that I had value and that it was okay to want to be seen.

In the course of my journey, I discovered that I needed to take care of me first to set an example, and let the rest naturally follow. The first step in my journey was to reclaim my inner child and forgive myself for all the imagined and exaggerated faults I feared that I had.

On your journey you will have days of pain and days of joy. It can be easy to forget the moments of joy when you are in the midst of the pain. Remember that the pain will pass and the joy will start to come more often. The hours or days of pain will become less overwhelming and less frequent. Both are necessary.

It is much like the blacksmiths who heat up the iron when shaping the horseshoe and then plunge it into the water to cool it. They reheat it again to make adjustments with a hammer and then cool it in order to create. The blacksmith repeats the process of heating and cooling until he creates the perfect horseshoe.

I tended to spend so much time working on and improving myself that I forgot to love myself. It all starts with self-love and filling yourself up so that you have enough for everyone else in your life. We cannot give from an empty tank. I continued to go through the motions of giving long after my tank was empty, but I think I would have served Davey better with a full tank.

The journey has not been a straight line. With all the zigs and zags, sometimes I felt like I was getting nowhere fast. And so it is with the inward journey. The quicksand, cliffs, and sand traps that lie in wait for us can seem overwhelming, but the only other choice is to do nothing.

And that will leave us where we were: unfulfilled and trying to make it through the day by overeating, drinking, and filling our days with meaningless entertainments, just to get through one more day.

As long as you have committed to the journey, trust in the process and know that you are moving forward. If all sorts of emotions are coming up, that is good. If you feel like you are going slightly crazy, that is even better because it means that you are bringing up major craploads from your past that you needed to process through.

Find a support system or accountability partner that will understand what you are going through and help keep you focused on your journey.

Takeaway:

Sometimes a leader needs to trust that she is moving in the right direction and not beat herself up. Taking time for herself is important and actually moves her forward towards her purpose.

Taking time for yourself is not a selfish act, but an act of self-love which frees you to love others even more. Remember that humor will always lighten the load along the way.

Stepping Stones:

When was the last time you enjoyed a belly laugh?

_____

_____

_____

_____

_____

_____

_____

When was the last time you laughed at yourself?

_____

_____

_____

_____

_____

_____

Where are you sabotaging yourself?

_____

_____

_____

_____

_____

Ask yourself what else you could learn from this.

_____

_____

_____

_____

_____

_____

Ask yourself what else this could mean.

_____

_____

_____

_____

_____

_____

CHAPTER 10

My Tummy Hurts

Practice Self-Love

Sometimes your tummy will hurt, and sometimes you will be so tired you won't know how to put one foot in front of the other. I would like to remind you that you need to pace yourself. If you need to rest, then rest. If you need to move forward, then move forward. If you need to write, then write. And if you need to go to the beach, then go to the beach. Don't overthink or overcomplicate things. This is not a sprint, it is a marathon. The world will change as each of us come on board. It is more a case of when each of us begins to "be" rather than necessarily what each of us do or accomplish.

The tipping point for change seems to come to an organization when just eleven percent of the people begin to believe in or support the change. Do we as women stand together for healing the planet? Even if we don't agree on how to do it, can we at least agree that something needs to change? Can we agree that we need to stand up and be counted? If we fail to stand up and be heard, then we are part of the problem in the world and not part of any solution.

When we change ourselves, we change the world.

When planning the Social Intelligence for Excellence program with Davey, I wasn't sure what Social Excellence would look like, so I began with one simple goal: honesty.

Being honest first with ourselves and then with others. This is what authenticity is all about on a fundamental level; however, when I wrote this program I had not had the benefit of years of personal development. I am still continuing to learn this more deeply on a daily basis.

The personal development work has helped put the definitions in place so that I understood what was meant by conditioned beliefs and lenses.

Davey and I started from a place where there were no written words or clear destination, so we wrote a Civil Code Program to at least define the starting point. I have always found that when something is written down and posted, everyone feels safer and the conflicts end because we have consensus on the working model of how we are going to live.

Civil Code Program
We Respect Ourselves
We Respect Others

RAW LEADERSHIP

We are cheerful
We are a family

Goal:
First: To be honest with ourselves about jobs, duties, and
responsibilities

Second: To be honest with others about needs, desires and
privileges that correspond

Fruition: *- honest adult relationships based on mature, mutual*
love and respect.

The conditioned beliefs and distorted lens that we look through are what causes the pain that we experience. The ego is in charge of the conditioned beliefs and it can be a merciless tyrant. Once we consciously begin to see reality, we can see what outcomes our actions create. Then we can intelligently choose to adapt our behaviors to get a different, more life-affirming outcome going forward.

This morning as I woke
The ego was playing
a drum solo in my brain
You like me,
know the beat
all the phrases that keep
us down and safe and dead inside.
as I work to start the syncopation of
competing thoughts to provide counterpoint to

the unrelenting ego storm.
I find the tears,
that threaten to come
even as I will them to the surface
remain locked not so deep inside
but so tantalizingly held back.
I will move about the day
feeling, knowing that this too
shall pass and I will again pick
up where I left off building
what has been the minor chord
up till now...the future where
I can stand tall and secure
knowing that I have
claimed all that is me.

The bottom line is to get in touch with your body, heart, and soul and begin to listen to what is being said. Your ego is the one that doesn't shut up. It will try to keep you small. Your heart and soul speak softly, but are trying to get you to shine.

Being grounded means becoming fully conscious and being fully present in the moment. Be very aware of what is happening right now. No matter what is going on, we can stay balanced, centered, and aligned with our soul and higher self. Then we will be able to control our reactive, knee jerk, and defensive behavioral patterns.

Being grounded can be a difficult task because we have an ego mind that likes to take us into the non-productive future thoughts of "What If". It takes us into the past of should have, could have, would have. Regrets, blame, and victim mentalities are no longer able to enslave when you are in the present. When our consciousness is fully in the present moment, we are very, very aware of everything happening within and around our being NOW. We can even be hyperaware of the core sensations in the body.

To instantly ground yourself, try standing barefoot on your lawn. Imagine the unwanted energy flowing into the ground. We are energy and we work best when the energy is grounded. Just like electricity works safely when grounded, when we ground the electrical boxes in our homes, we allow the energy to flow as it should.

Takeaway:

No one can go full steam ahead all of the time. We need to listen to our body and what it is telling us. Sometimes we need to hibernate and sometimes we need to charge ahead. Sometimes we need to zigzag, go over, around, or through.

Get creative and keep all options on the table. When your tummy hurts, it is a signal telling you to get grounded and immediately take care of yourself.

Stepping Stones:

When was the last time you did something to care for yourself?

_____

_____

_____

_____

_____

_____

_____

_____

_____

Practice grounding the next time you feel anxious, uneasy, frustrated, or upset. Notice what happens.

Name three things that you know replenish and revive you. If this seems like a tough question, then you really need to answer this. Now go do them!

CHAPTER 11

Giving Up

Forgive Yourself

Once we connect to our purpose, it does not matter what obstacles get in the way or how hard it is. We keep going until we accomplish it. Facing your fears one by one makes it easier to move forward and not quite so overwhelming.

Ky, my oldest grandson, is another mentor of mine. He is now in college and told me I could share this story. Ky's parents lived with us when he was born then moved out when he was two years old. Ky came back to live with us when he was five years old and finally was diagnosed with Asperger Syndrome. It was only after I removed him from the schools that they decided to finally test him.

When Ky came back to live with us, he would only eat pancakes with no brown spots... that was it! Needless to say, making pancakes without brown spots was not one of my fortes, so I decided to help him expand his food choices. One of the techniques I used with Davey, and now with Ky, was to talk it over with them when there was a change proposed. I wanted to get their agreement on what needed to be done.

I sat down with Ky and asked him if he wanted to learn how to enjoy other foods. You can imagine what he had to say... "No way!", so I sweetened the pot a little. If he would try ten new foods, I would take him to the Milwaukee museum for a day. He agreed. We also made a rule: he only had to take one bite of each food that was served, and if he didn't like it, he did not have to finish it.

If the same food was served at another meal, he needed to eat one bite again, but like before, he did not have to finish it. If he decided he liked something, then we celebrated and wrote the food on a chart that we posted on the wall. Throughout the day, I would remind him how proud I was of him and count up the number of foods that he liked.

If he forgot he liked one food that was served at a meal, then we referenced the chart to reassure him that he liked it. When we got to fifty items, we no longer needed the food chart. Today Ky eats everything and loves to try new foods. He even eats some foods I will not try!

When Ky was nine years old, his scout troop went to the local roller skating rink for an event. Ky had not been skating before, but said he did not need my help. I was helping his sister get her skates on when I heard a blood-curdling shriek. I looked up and saw Ky collapsed in the middle of the rink shrieking at the top of his lungs. He was having a meltdown. I rushed to his side as he screamed that skating was dumb and he was never doing it again. We removed his skates, but remained at the rink.

At this point, I realized that, while you do not need to learn to roller skate to be an adult, you do need to learn how to conquer the things that you fear; otherwise you will always be fearful and miss out on what life has to offer.

At home it took some talking, but Ky and I figured out how I could sweeten the pot so that he would give roller skating a try again. He agreed that, because I wanted him to learn, he would try again. This time he would hold my hand and go around the rink twice in order to get a quarter. The video game machine took two quarters, so in order to play a game he needed to go around the rink four times.

I had not been on skates in over thirty years and was not sure I could even stand, let alone skate; however, if he was game, then so was I. We began alternating between skating and gaming. After the video game, I would coax him back out to the rink to earn more quarters, and on it went. As we skated, I reminded him how well he was doing, and how much fun it is to roller skate.

It took three skating dates with me until Ky decided he could skate by himself. He told me, "It's okay, Grandma, I can do it." As I skated about ten feet behind him, I watched him not only skate, but add in some dance moves. He conquered fear that day!

I brushed tears from my eyes as I watched him cavort around the rink and knew we had accomplished much more than a simple skating lesson. We had learned a valuable life lesson that would form the foundation for future challenges.

At eighteen, he was already a published composer, artist, writer, Eagle Scout and so much more...

Where in your life are you letting the obstacles, real or imagined, stop you from achieving your dreams?

What if today you started taking the next step? Take just one simple, little step toward your future. You don't have to climb the mountain in one day.

Often in the past, I would question my decisions. I worried if I had gotten it "right". I wasted energy and stressed over "would-haves", "could-haves", and "should-haves". Sometimes it is not possible to know immediately whether a decision is right. I have needed to trust my gut and commit to the decision that I have made.

One decision, which I made years ago, took about two and a half years to manifest into a solid "yes". The level of commitment that I had to show in that situation is what finally brought the yes. If I had not committed to that decision, Davey would never have been able to write and express himself. That is a stunning thought! Perhaps making a decision or setting an intention creates the commitment to a goal or vision and that commitment brings about the "rightness"... in time.

Repeating the mantra "my mood or circumstances are immaterial" has helped me commit myself to the decisions I have made, knowing that the "rightness" will manifest itself in time.

Where in your life are you vacillating over a decision that you made, wondering if it was the correct decision for you? Is it time to recommit to that decision?

I have made decisions in my life that I questioned after the fact. I wondered what possessed me to make those particular "bad" decisions. Yet many of the decisions that others have looked at as bad or wrong decisions have actually been incredibly right.

One such decision was bringing Davey to Philadelphia to find out how to fix his seizure disorder. I spent five years of my life going through twice-yearly visits to learn the next steps to heal him. Davey was examined and measured so that we would know his starting point and take the next small steps toward health. After a week of lectures on the brain and human development, we would be given a new program to accomplish before the next visit, six months down the road.

The program was incredibly difficult and there were no breaks. The waiting list to get into the program was over a year long, and they did not put up with anyone who was not 100% committed to healing their child. That meant no days off for holidays, birthdays, or any other events or excuses. For this level of commitment, the payoff could be huge: a child who was well, seizure-free, happy, healthy, and living an abundant life.

For Davey, the steps of improvement came slowly at first, and they were hard for me to see. I was focused on the devastation of the seizures that ripped him apart. Davey crawled, crept, and wore a respiratory mask that forced him to breathe deeply and build up his respiratory muscles. One minute on, five minutes off, then repeat, over and over again until bedtime. We would wake up the next morning and start it all over again, but this relentless work slowly strengthened him.

Over that first year, he worked hard. He was detoxed from the deadly anticonvulsants that he had been put on to prevent the seizures, reducing them by half a dose a week. He started making progress: first reading books that I had written for him, then books by grade level, and soon he was reading beyond his years. He started running, brachiating arm over arm, and coming back to life. He still had seizures, but they were becoming fewer and farther apart.

During one visit, a few years into the program, they offered a new program that they had just developed: a positive respiratory machine that would reprogram his breathing and hopefully stop the seizures. It would require a higher level of commitment from us - it required that someone be awake twenty-four hours a day to watch the machine and monitor Davey.

We stepped up and made the commitment. In our first session that same day, we would be trained on the machine while we could be monitored. They set us up and Davey started his first session that afternoon.

I sat next to him and kept him entertained.

After thirty minutes on the machine, Davey picked up his pencil and wrote for the first time in his life. He was ten years old. He wrote his first words, a sentence that was completely backwards. The tears caught in my throat as I realized we had allowed him to use a previously inaccessible part of his brain.

I knew that my decision was the right one even when most people thought I was crazy to do what I had done. One of the hardest things I have had to learn was to let go of the things that were no longer serving me. I had to consciously drop old belief systems and outdated identities. In order to figure out what my belief systems were now, I had to break through my old conditioned beliefs.

In order to figure out what was important to me, I participated in an event by Dov Baron, one of the top 100 speakers on authentic leadership. At this event, I did an exercise to determine what was most important to me in my life. The top five things became my maxims on which I would base all my decisions. If it doesn't fit into what I have determined is important in my life, then the answer is no.

My maxims are:
1. Source/Creator/God
2. Being real/authentic (owning who I am and sharing it)
3. My health
4. My family (not just biological)
5. My business

When it came time for me to decide whether to stay in my marriage or leave it, the decision was not easy. I had been married for almost three decades. Since I started seriously working on myself again over the last few years, I had come to the conclusion that in order to really work on myself, I needed to leave my primary relationship. I had often wondered why "old" people would leave a relationship that they had been in for over a quarter of a century. To me it seemed pointless. Besides, I had stood before God and a priest and given the oath of "until death do us part". I had stayed because I said I would.

I finally realized that staying was not an option if being authentic was going to be my second highest maxim, coming only after God. I knew I could not be authentic to myself in this relationship. I needed to leave to give myself time to figure out where my path lay and to give my husband, James, the freedom to discover his own path. I walked forward in faith, knowing that it would become clearer as I moved.

It wasn't easy. It hurt tremendously, but I felt secure in the knowledge that this pain would end eventually and the future for both James and me would be good. In the end, I did what I believed was right, which is all anyone can do.

Is there anything in your life that you are holding onto out of obligation? What if blindly accepting where you are is keeping you stuck in the very place that is killing you?

One of the ways to move forward is to forgive yourself. Every place where you are stuck, forgive yourself for being stuck.

Forgive yourself for your anger and for not knowing the answers. In other words, forgive everything that you had a part in and everyone with whom you are angry. I had to forgive myself for Davey's death and for not staying in my marriage. I had believed I was not lovable, among many other things. Just forgive everything and take a load off your back to allow yourself to move forward.

Takeaway:

Once a leader is fully attached to her purpose, nothing will stop her from achieving it. Nothing will stand in her way. Obstacles will give way from the sheer strength of her resolve. Growth is what we are continually called to do.

Leaders embrace the pain, grow, and become agents of positive change in the world. We can heal the world, but only if we are willing to heal ourselves first.

<u>Stepping Stones:</u>

Who are you willing to be from this moment forward?

_____

_____

_____

_____

_____

_____

_____

What commitment do you need to make to yourself to make
this happen?

_____

_____

_____

_____

_____

_____

_____

_____

_____

_____

_____

_____

List five things you can do in the next week to begin creating this new version of yourself.

_____

_____

_____

_____

_____

_____

_____

_____

CHAPTER 12

Gratitude

Be Grateful

For me, gratitude had always felt like a powerless position. If you were grateful, I thought it meant that you were in a place where you were so desperate that you had no choice but to be grateful to others. I thought it meant you were so poor in a particular area, that you had to be given what you needed by someone else.

I felt that I had no power, even at times when others saw me as powerful. I did accomplish some things that seemed impossible at the time, but it did not feel that way to me. At the time, it was just about putting one foot in front of the other. I was focused only on doing the next thing that I had to do, or at least the next thing that I felt I had to do. Remember, our lives are really an outward expression of what is happening inside of us. It is always a matter of perspective.

Today I know that gratitude for all the things in my life is actually the fuel that is allowing my life to unfold as it should. As I remain grateful for all the things in my life, I am filled to the brim with all the possibilities that exist and with the promise of the future that is unfolding.

Neurologically, when we maintain a state of gratitude, we open new neural pathways and are more able to let go of old negative thinking. The brain cannot maintain two states of emotion at that same time. Staying in gratitude keeps the negative from being such a default mode. Remaining positive draws the positive to us. It really is that simple: what we think about, we bring about!

This is not saying that we walk around and ignore the chaos in our lives. Rather, we focus on the direction that we want to go so that we can create more of what we desire in our lives and less of the parts we don't want.

"Gratitude in our darkest times is more than a matter of remembering our blessings so we can hold the hard stuff in a bigger perspective. With understanding, we see that often it is the suffering itself that deepens us, maturing our perspective on life, making us more compassionate and wise than we would have been without it. How many times have we been inspired by those who embody a wisdom that could only come from dealing with adversity? And how many valuable lessons have we ourselves learned because life has given us unwanted challenges? With a grateful heart, we're not only willing to face our difficulties, we can realize while we're going through them that

they are a part of our ripening into wisdom and nobility."
—James Baraz, Awakening Joy[8]

An interesting word caught my attention a few years back: *dumbsaint.* It's such a strange word that, of course, I immediately looked it up. I found that a *dumbsaint* refers to a person of the mind to accept all things that happen.

It is someone who absorbs everything into his or her experience without any urge to change or correct. They have a complete understanding that all things happen and are happening, and they portray these things in the mind without judgment.

Choose to be a dumbsaint and the world becomes your banquet. There is a buffet of experience to be sampled with finger-licking delight when you don't have judgment and prejudice restricting your choices. Sadness, happiness, hard, easy, joy, laughter, and fun are all just choices on the buffet of life, all to be experienced in differing amounts depending on what we choose.

---

8 Baraz, James, and Shoshana Alexander. *Awakening Joy: 10 Steps That Will Put You on the Road to Real Happiness.* New York: Bantam, 2010. Print.

VICTORIA HARGIS

When I was young I dreamed a dream
Of being the Statue of Liberty
Standing tall to welcome
The tired, the poor,
huddled masses just
yearning to breathe free,
Considered the wretched refuse,
I would say
Send these, the homeless,
tempest-tossed, to me:
I lift my lamp to guide them home.
I stood strong battered by the waves
Crashing upon my feet
Refusing to give way
Determined to light
The way.
And then, in my dream, I got tired
And put the torch down
I have wondered over the years
At why I would put the torch down
It felt like giving up giving in
And I did not
Think I would ever
Give in give way
No matter how tired I was
This dream has stayed with me
over the years
The only one I remember still…
Having dreamed others I am sure
But they are gone
like whispers on the wind

RAW LEADERSHIP

Only this one stays...
And I think I am beginning to see this
Message over the years is there to
Light my way...
There is no shame in putting down the torch
That I have held over the years
Even Lady Liberty did in my dream
The shame would be in standing still
Only lighting the way
The shame would be in silently
Watching standing unmoved
Thinking; what can I do?
The Lady, a symbol of the possibilities
that await you when you break free
from all that is holding you back
and embrace the new, the promise.
This Lady Liberty has broken free
No longer held by the past chains
breaking free from
tyranny and the servitude
of disempowering beliefs
As they no longer
serve Me nor Thee.

Takeaway

A leader knows that staying in gratitude is a choice that smooths the path forward to leadership. It keeps you out of victim mode and provides you the ability to step into the life you want. There is always something to be grateful for.

Staying in gratitude keeps your mind from wallowing in the negative thoughts.

Stepping Stones:

What things are you grateful for in your life?

_____

_____

_____

_____

_____

_____

_____

_____

_____

If you can't think of anything, what would someone looking at your life say?

_____

_____

_____

_____

_____

_____

_____

_____

_____

_____

What would your neighbor or your family member say?

_____

_____

_____

_____

_____

_____

_____

_____

_____

_____

Gratitude needs to be part of your daily ritual and needs to be practiced.

Have you started your success journal yet?

CHAPTER 13

Fearless

Being Fearless

I received an unexpected surprise from my grandson Ky when he graduated from high school. We were talking about school and his plans for the future. He was about to be a freshman in college. I told him how proud I was of him and how far he had come. I told him to always reach for his dreams.

He replied, "You taught me to be fearless. I used to be afraid of everything, but you taught me to be fearless and now I don't fear anything."

My heart swelled. I was so honored that he thought that and that he was able to express what he was feeling. I wondered how I, who was so filled with fear, could have taught him to be fearless.

Then I remembered how he let me help him stand when he fell to the floor in total frustration, how he let me help him learn math, and how he trusted me to fix whatever difficulty he was in so he could start again. I had tried to honor him and his journey and to clear the path for him to have the space to become who he was meant to be.

Sometimes we need mentors that can see farther down the road than we can, simply by virtue of age or experience. In this case, my grandson was also my mentor. Everything I gave to him, I got back threefold.

He helped me see so many things differently. We have always had a special bond because he was willing to trust me and I was able to show him how much I valued him. I am deeply humbled and in awe of what he has already accomplished in his life.

Previously in my life, I would not move forward until I had researched something thoroughly, wanting to make sure that I knew all the pros and cons and had anticipated all the problems and issues that might come up. This felt like *paralysis by analysis*. I was really living in *fight or flight* mode. Sometimes this process kept me so quiet for so long, that I might have been mistaken for playing dead.

I have always loved it when kids start saying "No". That has always been my favorite stage for a kid: when they are full of themselves and try to control their surroundings. They shout their defiance to the world without a second thought about what anyone else thinks. I rejoiced when I first saw my kids assert their power and stand up for themselves. I know this is crazy-sounding since most people dread that stage in kids, but I would smile when a kid threw himself on the floor in Kmart or Walmart while having a temper tantrum.

The world seems to stop and wait for them, as if standing in wonderment at the sheer force of their want. Then the world (or the parents) would rush to stop them from acting in an embarrassing way in public. Sometimes nothing can stop their thunderous display of want. How gloriously alive they are during that time of their lives!

I took my two-year-old grandson, Kade, to a martial arts testing a few years ago and he enthusiastically participated from the sidelines. He yelled when the students yelled, clapped, and jumped up and down. He had never seen karate before. At one point he streaked across the dojo during a test because he wanted his boppa (his grandpa, James). Nothing would deter him from reaching James!

I had struggled to find that want in me, that incredible level of want that is so glorious and yet terrifying at the same time. I wondered sometimes if it got killed all those years ago, yet something in me refused to stop searching and looking, knowing that somewhere in me was the want. Something in me refused to let it go; something in me demanded expression.

Takeaway:

You will have fear and you can achieve everything you always wanted to have. When you connect to your desire with all the enthusiasm and emotion of a small child and take action the universe will work with you to accomplish those desires.

Stepping Stones:

What hopes do you harbor?

_____

_____

_____

_____

_____

_____

_____

_____

_____

_____

What dreams do you have?

_____

_____

_____

_____

_____

_____

_____

_____

_____

_____

_____

_____

VICTORIA HARGIS

_____

_____

_____

_____

_____

_____

_____

_____

_____

_____

_____

_____

_____

_____

_____

_____

_____

_____

_____

_____

_____

_____

_____

_____

_____

_____

_____

_____

VICTORIA HARGIS

———————————————

———————————————

———————————————

———————————————

———————————————

———————————————

———————————————

———————————————

———————————————

For me, I'm moving forward and trusting that my life is opening up to a new future. I am reminded daily that it is the small steps that I take every day that bring me to where I need to be. I don't always like the steps, but I am committed to making them. I am becoming aware on an ever deepening level and freeing myself of disempowering beliefs as they reveal themselves daily...

CHAPTER 14

Inspiration

Pulling It All Together

In contrast to the typical image of motherhood portrayed in greeting cards, the urban usage of the term "mommabear" is "a fierce protector". Throughout my journey to find my inner mommabear, I've been honored to connect to my highest purpose. Part of that is a relentless self-examination and a drive to smooth the way for others who may be going through difficulty or struggling to assert their voices.

I am grateful to have been able to share with you the lessons I received in becoming a mommabear leader and ferociously protecting the vulnerable. As women in the world, whether we are working for ourselves, in corporations, or at home, we cannot afford to quietly hibernate while those less-powerful (cubs) need us!

I was inspired to write this book to help women see the leader within, recognize potential mommabear moments, and use them to recreate themselves. Many of the existing leadership books left me cold and failed to address the distinctions between excellent female and male leaders.

Just as a thought experiment, close your eyes and picture a truck driver, a doctor, a pilot, or a CEO.

Chances are good that you pictured a male in those roles, based on our tendency as humans to generalize. While this can serve us well, extrapolating how to climb a whole flight based on the skills it took to climb a single step can also cause us to overlook alternatives.

When we refer to a woman who is a leader, we speak of a woman leader or a female leader, not using the general term leader.

I like to think that every person is made up of a spectrum containing both masculine and feminine energy. There are certain behaviors that each of us are capable of, and others that have been pre-assigned to either men or women. How do we allow space for another person's energy? Women can operate from their male energy as a driving force when they have too much to do and there is only one of them to get it done, but it can be hard to maintain that energy when it is not our default mode of operation.

New views of great leadership seem to highlight traits commonly ascribed to women such as empathy, relationship-building, and connecting. It is about accepting the duality that exists in each of us and allowing that duality to keep us grounded.

I struggled to accept my duality out of fear of powerlessness if I embraced femininity. My vision is to honor women in all their titles, wife, mother, single, crone, grandma, etc. and give them a voice that does justice to the range of energies required in that role.

There are many ways women may feel contained or temporarily silenced. Sometimes a woman's own fear of being perceived as aggressive can cause them to exaggerate their femininity or downplay their ideas.

Sometimes in our lives, something happens that shakes us awake to see more possibilities than we're currently experiencing. Remember that there are thousands of ways that your inner mommabear can awaken. Many women mistakenly believe they are just the secondary character in everyone else's life story. They dutifully attend to children and relentlessly seek out ways to keep the family running smoothly. When women share similar life experiences, it can construct an amazing connection between them and make them feel instant rapport.

When attempting to communicate with someone who doesn't have such obvious commonalities, it takes conscious work to avoid a disconnected feeling. For example, I had an interesting conversation with the leader of a group where I was a member. The two of us had a pattern of operating from old wounds instead of engaging in the issue at hand, detached from any previous failed communication attempts.

We were finally able to develop rapport by discussing the situation in private after the group disbanded. He apologetically referred to himself as "having to be right" and me as stubborn. I was able to emotionally detach from the label and look up the word to find adjectives that more accurately characterized me.

Stubbornness can be a good trait if it means we are persistently taking positive action and maintain a tenacious, unshakable frame of mind. It can also cause us problems if we apply that trait by showing rigidity where flexibility may work better, or if people perceive us as unreasonable.

Excellent leaders are stubborn about what they can take action on and flexible about what is not under their influence.

Because of my particular life experiences, I see the world through a lens that colors my views. As long as I am conscious of this bias, I can use it to my advantage. Then I can harness all the stubbornness I possess to fulfill my purpose and to lead. My mission is to help women locate their own turning point where they are no longer willing to accept what others tell them they are, where they are no longer willing to accept anything less than what is right for them.

> *"True leadership stems from individuality that is honestly, and sometimes imperfectly, expressed... Leaders should strive for authenticity over perfection."* —Sheryl Sandberg, COO of Facebook[9]

---

9 Sandberg, Sheryl, and Nell Scovell. *Lean In: Women, Work, and the Will to Lead.* N.p.: n.p., n.d. Print.

Psychologist and human resources consultant, Professor Michele Paludi, notes women's management styles tend to be less hierarchical, more team-oriented, more flexible, and solicitous of other's opinions. This can be a tremendous strength in to-day's fast-changing business environments, as long as it isn't misconstrued as indecisiveness.

Trying to counteract that stereotype by being more assertive may also be seen as overly demanding. Paludi observed that the studies indicated that no matter what you do, you will be criticized. This makes it even more critical for a female leader to maintain the mindset of stubbornly rejecting conclusions or plans that don't feel right.

The abundance of labels placed on women, especially applied to public figures, can make it difficult to own who we really are, but once we are clear on our convictions, we will be able to lead decisively. Mothers can be especially resourceful in creatively employing all of their skills to do whatever it takes to accom-plish their goals for their children. How we label ourselves more powerfully shapes our lives than anything another person could ever say about us! Men and women stepping up and sharing their unique gifts will create the world they want to live in.

For women, the already difficult task of making sense of the roles they want is often complicated by social norms that task young girls with babysitting and caring for the needs of others, even at very young ages. That pressure to care for younger chil-dren can overwhelm some women, especially if they are also still working on their own self-care and working through the all too common human condition issues such as depression.

On an airplane, they tell you to put on your own oxygen mask before you take care of anyone else. It benefits everyone to practice self-love and invest time to first figure out your higher purpose before devoting all energies to serving the needs of others. A strong leader is able to inspire others precisely because they have already done the self-examination work behind the scenes that revealed their vision for a compelling future. If this process is rushed, the result can be exhaustion and the inability to decisively make changes that could result in better situations.

> *"A woman with a voice is by definition a strong woman, but the search to find that voice can be remarkably difficult."*
> —Melinda Gates

When the woman awakens, she becomes a powerful, self-directed leader of her own life. Then she becomes an agent of change in the world around her, whether mainly within her own community, or on a global scale. This change is triggered when the circumstantial evidence that something is not quite right with the world she is living in grows to the point where she can no longer ignore it. At that point, she either allows the inner mommabear to take over or she slides into a comfortable depression and lives out the rest of her life in resignation to her situation and whatever circumstances those around her are in.

My mommabear was first triggered when I realized that my youngest son, Davey, had a chance to get well. I had been told by the doctors that I should put him on a series of anticonvulsants to control his seizure disorder and I dutifully followed their instructions. Then I went to the Institute for Human Potential and learned that the brain grows by use and that past results do not need to dictate future results. What was before does not need to be what will be.

This philosophy allowed me the freedom to create a life for Davey that gave him a life well-lived. It opened my eyes to a wider range of possibilities. It allowed him to have a more full experience of the human condition that wasn't so heavily skewed by the chemical side effects of living in a heavily medicated state.

Once a woman connects with her inner mommabear, she becomes unstoppable. Think of all the powerful women in the world who have made a difference. Each of these women had a moment where they were tested and made the decision to step up and fulfill their purpose. Nothing stopped them and they worked tirelessly towards their vision.

Women who connected with their inner mommabear and exemplified fearless leadership:

Jane Addams *(1860-1935)* was a pioneer American settlement social worker, philosopher, author, leader in women's suffrage and world peace. She lived during the time of Theodore Roosevelt and Woodrow Wilson. Jane helped to turn America's attention to the plight of mothers working on the needs of children, local public health, and world peace.

Jane worked to give women the right to vote, founded Hull House, and was a co-founder of the ACLU (American Civil

Liberties Union). She was the first American woman to receive the Nobel Peace Prize and is noted as the founder of the American social work profession.

A defining mommabear moment for her appears to have come on a trip to Europe when she was twenty-seven. She attended a bullfight that was filled with pageantry and excitement. Later, as she reflected on the experience, she was horrified and ashamed at her lack of compassion for the horses and bulls that died from their wounds that day. Her thoughts then turned to the aimlessness of her life that seemed to consist of idle days filled with no purpose.

She immediately pledged to exercise her intelligence and creativity on behalf of the urban poor. Less than two years later, she opened Hull House, a Chicago community center of university women who created educational opportunities for struggling European immigrants.

Maria Corazon "Cory" Aquino *(1923-2009)* served as the first woman president of the Philippines and the first female president in all of Asia. She strongly emphasized the importance of civil liberties and human rights, and was instrumental in peace talks to resolve Communist insurgency and Islamist secession movements. She worked to restore economic health and confidence and focused on creating a market-oriented economy that was still socially responsible.

She was the most prominent figure of the 1986 People Power Revolution that successfully toppled the twenty year dictatorship of President Ferdinand Marcos, restoring democracy to the Philippines. President Marcos was known for corruption, extravagance, and brutality.

This self-proclaimed "plain housewife" was married to Senator Benigno Aquino, Jr., the staunchest critic of President Marcos. Her mommabear moment appears to have come when her husband was assassinated on August 21, 1983. This happened just as he was returning to the Philippines from exile in the United States. Less than two years later she ran for the presidency against Marcos.

After the 1986 elections were held on February 7th, the National Assembly proclaimed Marcos and his running mate as the winners, despite allegations of voter fraud. Aquino called for massive civil disobedience and led the People Power Revolution that ousted Marcos and secured her accession on February 25, 1986.

Marie Curie *(1867-1934)* discovered the radioactive element radium. She was the first person ever to win two Nobel Prizes and was one of only two people to win in more than one scientific field. Her influence on society could be compared to Albert Einstein in its reach. Her discoveries helped lead to the development of cancer treatments, X-rays, nuclear energy, sterilization of medical instruments, and even treatments for blindness. She found elements that were transforming matter into energy and pioneered medical uses of uranium, helping prevent infection for over a million wounded soldiers during World War I.

Early in her life she lost one sister to typhus and her mother died of tuberculosis. Grieving may have caused young Marie to turn her passion to understanding things from a scientific, rather than religious, perspective. Marie was unwilling to accept such tragedies as God's will.

Sandra Day O'Connor *(1930-present)* graduated from law school to discover that no law firm would offer her a job except as a legal secretary. She refused to settle and turned to public service as a Deputy County Attorney, Assistant Attorney General in Arizona, State Senator, County Superior Court judge, Arizona Court of Appeals, and finally as a United States Supreme Court Judge. She was the first woman to serve as Supreme Court justice in the 191-year history of the United States. Sandra is respected for being both fiercely independent and fair.

Rosa Parks *(1913-2005)* was asked to give up her seat on a bus to a white man and refused. Parks had not planned the protest, but "had been pushed as far as I could stand to be pushed." She couldn't take it anymore and said, "It is such a long and lonely feeling. The line between reason and madness grows thinner (due to the) horrible restrictiveness of Jim Crow laws."

And so she decided to withdraw her participation in the current system of degradation. Parks felt she was being asked to consent to her own humiliation: "I felt that, if I did not stand up, it meant that I approved of the way I was being treated, and I did not approve." Tired of giving in, Mrs. Parks had reached her mommabear moment. Rosa thought about her grandfather keeping his gun to protect their family and decided to stand fast. "People always say that I didn't give up my seat because I was tired, but that isn't true. I was not tired physically, or no more tired than I usually was at the end of a working day… No, the only tired I was, was tired of giving in." Her refusal to give in sparked a boycott of the bus company that lasted over a year. Rosa became a symbol of the civil rights movement.

Eleanor Roosevelt *(1884-1962)* began to give speeches, write articles, and make guest appearances on the radio to earn money for her family when her husband became sick with polio. By working in the UN, she was able to defend human rights. Her husband's affair was another motivation for Eleanor Roosevelt because it caused her to become more independent. Eleanor was also motivated by how hard it was for people during the Great Depression and the Second World War. She was moved to help.

Margaret Sanger *(1879-1966)* was a birth control activist, sex educator, and nurse. She founded an organization that later became Planned Parenthood. After graduating from college, Margaret took a teaching position in New Jersey until she was forced to return home to care for her dying mother. Her mother's death in 1896 was her mommabear moment and left her with a deep sense of dissatisfaction concerning her own and society's medical ignorance. Soon afterward, Margaret moved to White Plains, New York, where she trained as a nurse. She then moved to New York City and served in the extremely poor conditions of the slums.

Senator Elizabeth Warren *(1949-present)* from Massachusetts, is most famous for questioning big banking's irresponsibility in the economic crisis of 2008. She recently published a book of memoirs, *A Fighting Chance*, linking her upbringing by struggling middle-class parents with her political views. She especially spoke for tougher policing of Wall Street, higher minimum wages, expanded Social Security benefits, cheaper loans for college students, and protecting union organizing and collective bargaining.

Harriet Tubman *(1822-1913)* was born into slavery. The violence she suffered early in life caused permanent physical injuries and a lifetime of seizures. By the time Harriet became an adult, around half of the African-American people on the eastern shore of Maryland were free.

In fact, her own family contained both slave and free members. Her own mommabear moment came when Harriet escaped from slavery in 1849, fleeing to Philadelphia. Tubman decided to escape following a bout of illness and the death of her owner in 1849. She feared that her family would be sold off, and feared for own her fate as a sickly slave of low economic value. Harriet had no plans to remain in bondage, she soon set off alone for Pennsylvania.

Caitlyn Jenner *(1949-present)* was born in a male body. Caitlyn made a courageous choice to become the woman she always felt she was. She waited until she was in her sixties, after trying to live life as her originally-assigned birth gender. Caitlyn's transformation gives us a glimpse into how genders are treated in the media and in society.

Oprah Winfrey *(1954 -present)* defied the odds of succeeding in television as a black woman. One of her mommabear moments came when she made the risky decision to change the direction of her show. Instead of engaging in the race to the bottom, she embraced her identity, and decided to empower women with her public forum.

Every woman who has ever lived has made some sort of difference in the lives of others. The amount of difference will be determined by whether they have faced their mommabear moments and consciously shifted to living with purpose or whether they passively avoided any challenges that appeared too hard, sleepwalking through life.

Women's hopes, dreams, and desires have a far greater impact than you can imagine.

The world is waiting for each of us to step up. Your gift and purpose is a necessary part of the mosaic of the world.

There is a purpose for all of us. Every human being has value and purpose. We must become awake and aware to be in tune with our calling.

In order to speak up, you need the oxygen. So put the mask on your face first and breathe deep. Heal yourself so you can help heal the world. Consciously accelerate down your path to become the leader you were born to be.

I am reminded to thank the people in my life that are supporting and helping my dream move forward. Thank you to all those that share and comment in social media and call me on my s***. I appreciate all those that encourage, smile, and talk to me. Thank you to those that teach, learn from me, and those who just hold me in their thoughts. I love you and thank you with all of my heart.

An offer of help

If I can be of service to you on your quest to bring out your inner mommabear and go from Stuck to Spectacular by awakening your power within, please reach out to me through my website: http://www.victoriahargis.com

Need a Speaker?
Email me at: Victoria@victoriahargis.com

Visit my website:
Go to www.victoriahargis.com/bookgift to download a special gift I prepared for you to help you in your quest toward raw leadership.

Connect with me on social media:
Facebook: facebook.com/author.victoria.hargis
LinkedIn: linkedin.com/in/victoriahargis1
Twitter: twitter.com/victoriahargis

Join my Facebook group Soul Driven Women Entrepreneur at http://www.facebook.com/groups/souldriven